The
GOD-DEPENDENT
Woman

Life Choices from Second Corinthians

Learn to rely on God in a messy world

MELANIE NEWTON

We extend our heartfelt thanks to the women who served as editors for this study guide: Michelle Burns, Heather Newton, Sharon Edwards, Kristin Martin, Julia Gendron, Bethany Hayward, Marlo Brazeal, Trina Stephens, Monica Rice, Marlyn Scott, Melodye Carlock, and Kim Newton. Without such wonderful help, we would never have accomplished this monumental task in a timely manner. Your work is much appreciated.

The God-Dependent Woman: Life Choices from Second Corinthians

© 2025 Melanie Newton. All rights reserved.

Published by Joyful Walk Press. Flower Mound, TX.

ISBN: 978-0-9978703-9-8

For questions about the use of this study guide or for bulk orders, please email us at melanienewton.com/contact.

Cover design graphic is "anemone-3616880_1920.jpg" a public domain image by Mabel Amber on pixabay.com.

> Scripture quotations indicated NIV are taken from the Holy Bible, New International Version ®, NIV ®. Copyright © 1973, 1978, 1984, 2011 by International Bible Society. Used by permission of Zondervan Publishing Company. All rights reserved.

Melanie Newton is the author of "Graceful Beginnings" books for anyone new to the Bible and "Joyful Walk Bible Studies" for established Christians. Her mission is to help women learn to study the Bible for themselves and to grow their Bible-teaching skills to lead others.

Joyful Walk Bible Studies are grace-based studies for women of all ages. Each study guide follows the inductive method of Bible study (observation, interpretation, application) in a warm and inviting format.

We pray that you and your group will find *The God-Dependent Woman* a resource that God will use to strengthen you in your faith walk with Him.

Christ-Focused • Bible-Rich • Grace-Based

MELANIE NEWTON

Melanie Newton is a Louisiana girl who made the choice to follow Jesus while attending LSU. She and her husband Ron married and moved to Texas for him to attend Dallas Theological Seminary. They stayed in Texas where Ron led a wilderness camping ministry for troubled youth for many years. Ron now helps corporations with their challenging employees and is the author of the top-rated business book, *No Jerks on the Job*.

Melanie jumped into raising three Texas-born children and serving in ministry to women at her church. Through the years, the Lord has given her opportunity to do Bible teaching and to write grace-based Bible studies for women that are now available from her website (melanienewton.com) and on Bible.org. *Graceful Beginnings* books are for anyone new to the Bible. *Joyful Walk Bible Studies* are for maturing Christians.

Melanie Newton loves to help women learn how to study the Bible for themselves. She also teaches online courses for women to grow their Bible-teaching skills to help others—all with the goal of getting to know Jesus more along the way. Her heart's desire is to encourage you to have a joyful relationship with Jesus Christ so you are willing to share that experience with others around you.

> "Jesus took hold of me in 1972, and I have been on this great adventure ever since. My life is a gift of God, full of blessings in the midst of difficult challenges. The more I have learned and experienced God's absolutely amazing grace, the more I have discovered my faith walk to be a joyful one. I'm still seeking that joyful walk every day…"
>
> *Melanie*

OTHER BIBLE STUDIES BY MELANIE NEWTON

Graceful Beginnings books for anyone new to the Bible:
- A Fresh Start (basics for new Christians)
- Painting the Portrait of Jesus (the Gospel of John)
- The God You Can Know (the character of God)
- Grace Overflowing (an overview of Paul's 13 letters)
- The Walk from Fear to Faith (7 Old Testament women)
- Satisfied by His Love (women who knew Jesus)
- Seek the Treasure (study of Ephesians)
- Pathways to a Joyful Walk (6 pathways to a life filled with joy)

Joyful Walk Bible Studies for growing Christians:
- Adorn Yourself with Godliness (1 Timothy and Titus, also in Spanish)
- Everyday Women, Ever Faithful God (Old Testament women, also in Spanish)
- Connecting Faith to Life on Planet Earth (Genesis 1-11; Revelation)
- Graceful Living (the essentials for a grace-based Christian life)
- Graceful Living Today (a devotional journal for a joyful life)
- Healthy Living (Colossians and Philemon)
- Heartbreak to Hope (the Gospel of Mark)
- Identity: Sticking to Your Faith in a Pull-Apart World (Ezra thru Malachi)
- Knowing Jesus, Knowing Joy (Philippians, also in Spanish)
- Live Out His Love (New Testament women)
- Perspective (1and 2 Thessalonians)
- Profiles of Perseverance (Old Testament men, also in Spanish)
- Radical Acts (Acts)
- Reboot, Renew, Rejoice (1 and 2 Chronicles)
- The God-Dependent Woman (2 Corinthians)
- To Be Found Faithful (2 Timothy)

Resources for leading others
- Be a Christ-Focused Small Group Leader
- Leap into Lifestyle Disciplemaking
- Bible Study Leadership Made Easy (online video course)
- Painting the Picture of Jesus (the "I Am's" of Jesus lessons for children)
- Teaching Children the God They Can Know (the character of God for children)

Download our catalogue and get more resources for your spiritual growth at melanienewton.com.

Contents

INTRODUCTION

Using This Study Guide 1

Second Corinthians (NIV 2011) 3

LESSONS

1: The God on Whom We Can Rely (1:1-11) 13

2: Promises and Faithfulness (1:12-2:13) 27

3: Connect and Impart for God's Glory (2:14-4:6) 41

4: Let God's Light Shine (4:7-5:10) 57

5: Your Life Has Purpose (5:11-6:10) 71

6: Open Wide Your Hearts (6:11-7:16) 85

7: Generosity from Joy Overflowing (8:1-9:15) 101

8: Tearing Down Walls (10:1-18) 117

9: Live to Serve Christ through Anything (11:1-33) 133

10: Dependent Living Is Powerful (12:1-21) 151

11: Christ Is All We Need for Life (13:1-14) 167

RESOURCES

Why Depend on God More than on Yourself 179

Ways to Explain the Gospel 182

Small Group Discussion Guide 185

INTRODUCTION

Using This Study Guide

This study guide consists of 11 lessons covering Paul's letter we know as "Second Corinthians." Since this letter consists of 13 chapters in our New Testaments, we will need to cover more than one chapter in some of the lessons. The lessons are divided into 5 sections (about 25 minutes in length). The first 4 sections contain a detail study of the Bible verses. The fifth section is a podcast that provides additional insight to the lesson. If you cannot do the entire lesson one week, please read the Bible passage covered by the lesson and try to do the "Day One Study" of the lesson.

THE BASIC STUDY

Each lesson includes core questions covering the passage narrative. These core questions will take you through the process of inductive Bible study—observation, interpretation, and application. It is the best approach for doing Bible Study. The process is more easily understood in the context of answering these questions:

- What does the Bible say? *(Observation: what's in the text)*
- What does it mean? *(Interpretation: the author's intended meaning)*
- How does this apply to me today? *(Application: making it personal)*

STUDY ENHANCEMENTS

Dependent Living ✽*:* The focus of this study is choices we make to rely more on God than on ourselves in weakness and in strength. That is called dependent living, meaning we live in daily dependence upon God. Some questions have a DL ✽ in front of them. These will prompt you to recognize what it means to live dependently on God and how to apply it to your life.

Study Aids: To aid in proper interpretation and application of the study, additional study aids are located where appropriate in the lesson:

- Historical Insights
- Scriptural Insights
- From the Greek (definitions of Greek words)
- Focus on the Meaning
- Think About It (thoughtful reflection)

Other useful study tools: Use online tools or apps (blueletterbible.org or "Blue Letter Bible app" is especially helpful) to find *cross references* (verses with similar content to what you are studying) and meanings of the *original Greek words or phrases* used (usually called "interlinear"). You can also look at any verse in *various Bible translations* to help with understanding what it is saying. You will have the opportunity to add your own study at the end of every **What does it mean?** section.

PODCASTS

Find podcasts for these lessons at melanienewton.com/podcasts (choose "8: 2 Corinthians) and on most podcast providers. Or you can read the blogs associated with the podcasts at melanienewton.com/blog. Choose 2 Corinthians category then scroll to find the title you want. Listen to the first podcast as an introduction to the study.

New Testament Summary

The New Testament opens with the births of Jesus and John (often called "the baptist"). About 30 years later, John challenged the Jews to indicate their repentance (turning from sin and toward God) by submitting to water baptism—a familiar Old Testament practice used for repentance as well as when a Gentile converted to Judaism (to be washed clean of idolatry).

Jesus Christ, God's incarnate Son, publicly showed the world what God is like and taught His perfect ways for 3 – 3½ years. After preparing 12 disciples to continue Christ's earthly work, He died voluntarily on a cross for mankind's sin, rose from the dead, and returned to heaven. The account of His earthly life is recorded in 4 books known as the Gospels (the biblical books of Matthew, Mark, Luke and John named after the compiler of each account).

After Jesus' return to heaven, the followers of Christ were then empowered by the Holy Spirit and spread God's salvation message among the Jews, a number of whom believed in Christ. The apostle Paul and others traveling with him carried the good news to the Gentiles during 3 missionary journeys (much of this recorded in the book of Acts). Paul wrote 13 New Testament letters to churches and individuals (Romans through Philemon). The section in our Bible from Hebrews to Jude contains 8 additional letters penned by five men, including two apostles (Peter and John) and two of Jesus' half-brothers (James and Jude). The author of Hebrews is unknown. The apostle John also recorded Revelation, which summarizes God's final program for the world. The Bible ends as it began—with a new, sinless creation.

Discussion Group Guidelines

Anyone can do this study alone. If you are doing this as part of a group, we suggest you use the following guidelines to maintain a safe environment for your group members to learn together.

1. **Attend consistently** whether your lesson is done or not. You will learn from the other women, and they want to get to know you.
2. **Set aside time** to work through the study questions. The goal of Bible study is to **get to know** Jesus. He will change your life.
3. **Share your insights** from your personal study time. As you spend time in the Bible, Jesus will teach you truth through His Spirit inside you.
4. **Respect each other's insights**. Listen thoughtfully. Encourage each other as you interact. Refrain from dominating the discussion if you have a tendency to be talkative. ☺
5. **Celebrate our unity** in Christ. Avoid bringing up controversial subjects such as politics, divisive issues, and denominational differences.
6. **Maintain confidentiality.** Remember that anything shared during the group time is not to leave the **group** (unless permission is granted by the one sharing).
7. **Pray for one another** as sisters in Christ.
8. **Get to know the women** in your group. Please do not use your small group members for solicitation purposes for home businesses, though.

There is a small group discussion guide available at the end of this study. Anyone can use the guide to lead a group through a discussion of the questions in this study. This is especially useful for groups that have less than two hours to meet together.

Enjoy your Joyful Walk Bible Study!

Second Corinthians

New International Version (2011)

Paul, an apostle of Christ Jesus by the will of God, and Timothy our brother,

To the church of God in Corinth, together with all his holy people throughout Achaia:

Grace and peace to you from God our Father and the Lord Jesus Christ.

Praise be to the God and Father of our Lord Jesus Christ, the Father of compassion and the God of all comfort, who comforts us in all our troubles, so that we can comfort those in any trouble with the comfort we ourselves receive from God. For just as we share abundantly in the sufferings of Christ, so also our comfort abounds through Christ. If we are distressed, it is for your comfort and salvation; if we are comforted, it is for your comfort, which produces in you patient endurance of the same sufferings we suffer. And our hope for you is firm, because we know that just as you share in our sufferings, so also you share in our comfort.

We do not want you to be uninformed, brothers and sisters, about the troubles we experienced in the province of Asia. We were under great pressure, far beyond our ability to endure, so that we despaired of life itself. Indeed, we felt we had received the sentence of death. But this happened that we might not rely on ourselves but on God, who raises the dead. He has delivered us from such a deadly peril, and he will deliver us again. On him we have set our hope that he will continue to deliver us, as you help us by your prayers. Then many will give thanks on our behalf for the gracious favor granted us in answer to the prayers of many.

Now this is our boast: Our conscience testifies that we have conducted ourselves in the world, and especially in our relations with you, with integrity and godly sincerity. We have done so, relying not on worldly wisdom but on God's grace. For we do not write you anything you cannot read or understand. And I hope that, as you have understood us in part, you will come to understand fully that you can boast of us just as we will boast of you in the day of the Lord Jesus.

Because I was confident of this, I wanted to visit you first so that you might benefit twice. I wanted to visit you on my way to Macedonia and to come back to you from Macedonia, and then to have you send me on my way to Judea. Was I fickle when I intended to do this? Or do I make my plans in a worldly manner so that in the same breath I say both "Yes, yes" and "No, no"?

But as surely as God is faithful, our message to you is not "Yes" and "No." For the Son of God, Jesus Christ, who was preached among you by us—by me and Silas and Timothy—was not "Yes" and "No," but in him it has always been "Yes." For no matter how many promises God has made, they are "Yes" in Christ. And so through him the "Amen" is spoken by us to the glory of God. Now it is God who makes both us and you stand firm in Christ. He anointed us, set his seal of ownership on us, and put his Spirit in our hearts as a deposit, guaranteeing what is to come.

I call God as my witness—and I stake my life on it—that it was in order to spare you that I did not return to Corinth. Not that we lord it over your faith, but we work with you for your joy, because it is by faith you stand firm.

So I made up my mind that I would not make another painful visit to you. For if I grieve you, who is left to make me glad but you whom I have grieved? I wrote as I did, so that when I came I would not be distressed by those who should have made me rejoice. I had confidence in all of you, that you would all share my joy. For I wrote you out of great distress and anguish of heart and with many tears, not to grieve you but to let you know the depth of my love for you.

If anyone has caused grief, he has not so much grieved me as he has grieved all of you to some extent—not to put it too severely. The punishment inflicted on him by the majority is sufficient. Now instead, you ought to forgive and comfort him, so that he will not be overwhelmed by excessive sorrow. I urge you, therefore, to reaffirm your love for him. Another reason I wrote you was to see if you would stand the test and be obedient in everything. Anyone you forgive, I also forgive. And what I have forgiven—if there was anything to forgive—I have forgiven in the sight of Christ for your sake, in order that Satan might not outwit us. For we are not unaware of his schemes.

Now when I went to Troas to preach the gospel of Christ and found that the Lord had opened a door for me, I still had no peace of mind, because I did not find my brother Titus there. So I said goodbye to them and went on to Macedonia.

But thanks be to God, who always leads us as captives in Christ's triumphal procession and uses us to spread the aroma of the knowledge of him everywhere. For we are to God the pleasing aroma of Christ among those who are being saved and those who are perishing. To the one we are an aroma that brings death; to the other, an aroma that brings life. And who is equal to such a task? Unlike so many, we do not peddle the word of God for profit. On the contrary, in Christ we speak before God with sincerity, as those sent from God.

Are we beginning to commend ourselves again? Or do we need, like some people, letters of recommendation to you or from you? You yourselves are our letter, written on our hearts, known and read by everyone. You show that you are a letter from Christ, the result of our ministry, written not with ink but with the Spirit of the living God, not on tablets of stone but on tablets of human hearts.

Such confidence we have through Christ before God. Not that we are competent in ourselves to claim anything for ourselves, but our competence comes from God. He has made us competent as ministers of a new covenant—not of the letter but of the Spirit; for the letter kills, but the Spirit gives life.

Now if the ministry that brought death, which was engraved in letters on stone, came with glory, so that the Israelites could not look steadily at the face of Moses because of its glory, transitory though it was, will not the ministry of the Spirit be even more glorious? If the ministry that brought condemnation was glorious, how much more glorious is the ministry that brings righteousness! For what was glorious has no glory now in comparison with the surpassing glory. And if what was transitory came with glory, how much greater is the glory of that which lasts!

Therefore, since we have such a hope, we are very bold. We are not like Moses, who would put a veil over his face to prevent the Israelites from seeing the end of what was passing away. But their minds were made dull, for to this day the same veil remains when the old covenant is read. It has not been removed, because only in Christ is it taken away. Even to this day when Moses is read, a veil covers their hearts. But whenever anyone turns to the Lord, the veil is taken away. Now the Lord is the Spirit, and where the Spirit of the Lord is, there is freedom. And we all, who with unveiled faces contemplate the Lord's glory, are being transformed into his image with ever-increasing glory, which comes from the Lord, who is the Spirit.

Therefore, since through God's mercy we have this ministry, we do not lose heart. Rather, we have renounced secret and shameful ways; we do not use deception, nor do we distort the word of God. On the contrary, by setting forth the truth plainly we commend ourselves to everyone's conscience in the sight of God. And even if our gospel is veiled, it is veiled to those who are perishing. The god of this age has blinded the minds of unbelievers, so that they cannot see the light of the gospel that displays the glory of Christ, who is the image of God. For what we preach is not ourselves, but Jesus Christ as Lord, and ourselves as your servants for Jesus' sake. For God, who said, "Let light shine out of darkness," made his light shine in our hearts to give us the light of the knowledge of God's glory displayed in the face of Christ.

But we have this treasure in jars of clay to show that this all-surpassing power is from God and not from us. We are hard pressed on every side, but not crushed; perplexed, but not in despair; persecuted, but not abandoned; struck down, but not destroyed. We always carry around in our body the death of Jesus, so that the life of Jesus may also be revealed in our body. For we who are alive are always being given over to death for Jesus' sake, so that his life may also be revealed in our mortal body. So then, death is at work in us, but life is at work in you.

It is written: "I believed; therefore I have spoken." Since we have that same spirit of faith, we also believe and therefore speak, because we know that the one who raised the Lord Jesus from the dead will also raise us with Jesus and present us with you to himself. All this is for your benefit, so that the grace that is reaching more and more people may cause thanksgiving to overflow to the glory of God.

Therefore we do not lose heart. Though outwardly we are wasting away, yet inwardly we are being renewed day by day. For our light and momentary troubles are achieving for us an eternal glory that far outweighs them all. So we fix our eyes not on what is seen, but on what is unseen, since what is seen is temporary, but what is unseen is eternal.

For we know that if the earthly tent we live in is destroyed, we have a building from God, an eternal house in heaven, not built by human hands. Meanwhile we groan, longing to be clothed instead with our heavenly dwelling, because when we are clothed, we will not be found naked. For while we are in this tent, we groan and are burdened, because we do not wish to be unclothed but to be clothed instead with our heavenly dwelling, so that what is mortal may be swallowed up by life. Now the one who has fashioned us for this very purpose is God, who has given us the Spirit as a deposit, guaranteeing what is to come.

Therefore we are always confident and know that as long as we are at home in the body we are away from the Lord. For we live by faith, not by sight. We are confident, I say, and would prefer to be away from the body and at home with the Lord. So we make it our goal to please him, whether we are at home in the body or away from it. For we must all appear before the judgment seat of Christ, so that each of us may receive what is due us for the things done while in the body, whether good or bad.

Since, then, we know what it is to fear the Lord, we try to persuade others. What we are is plain to God, and I hope it is also plain to your conscience. We are not trying to commend ourselves to you again, but are giving you an opportunity to take pride in us, so that you can answer those who take pride in what is seen rather than in what is in the heart. If we are "out of our mind," as some say, it is for God; if we are in our right mind, it is for you. For Christ's love compels us, because we are convinced that one died for all, and therefore all died. And he died for all, that those who live should no longer live for themselves but for him who died for them and was raised again.

So from now on we regard no one from a worldly point of view. Though we once regarded Christ in this way, we do so no longer. Therefore, if anyone is in Christ, the new creation has come: The old has gone, the new is here! All this is from God, who reconciled us to himself through Christ and gave us the ministry of reconciliation: that God was reconciling the world to himself in Christ, not counting people's sins against them. And he has committed to us the message of reconciliation. We are therefore Christ's ambassadors, as though God were making his appeal through us. We implore you on Christ's behalf: Be reconciled to God. God made him who had no sin to be sin for us, so that in him we might become the righteousness of God.

As God's co-workers we urge you not to receive God's grace in vain. For he says, "In the time of my favor I heard you, and in the day of salvation I helped you." I tell you, now is the time of God's favor, now is the day of salvation.

We put no stumbling block in anyone's path, so that our ministry will not be discredited. Rather, as servants of God we commend ourselves in every way: in great endurance; in troubles, hardships and distresses; in beatings, imprisonments and riots; in hard work, sleepless nights and hunger; in purity, understanding, patience and kindness; in the Holy Spirit and in sincere love; in truthful speech and in the power of God; with weapons of righteousness in the right hand and in the left; through glory and dishonor, bad report and good report; genuine, yet regarded as impostors; known, yet regarded as unknown; dying, and yet we live on; beaten, and yet not killed; sorrowful, yet always rejoicing; poor, yet making many rich; having nothing, and yet possessing everything.

We have spoken freely to you, Corinthians, and opened wide our hearts to you. We are not withholding our affection from you, but you are withholding yours from us. As a fair exchange—I speak as to my children—open wide your hearts also.

Do not be yoked together with unbelievers. For what do righteousness and wickedness have in common? Or what fellowship can light have with darkness? What harmony is there between Christ and Belial? Or what does a believer have in common with an unbeliever? What agreement is there between the temple of God and idols? For we are the temple of the living God. As God has said:

"I will live with them and walk among them, and I will be their God, and they will be my people."

Therefore, "Come out from them and be separate, says the Lord. Touch no unclean thing, and I will receive you."

And, "I will be a Father to you, and you will be my sons and daughters, says the Lord Almighty."

Therefore, since we have these promises, dear friends, let us purify ourselves from everything that contaminates body and spirit, perfecting holiness out of reverence for God.

Make room for us in your hearts. We have wronged no one, we have corrupted no one, we have exploited no one. I do not say this to condemn you; I have said before that you have such a place in our hearts that we would live or die with you. I have spoken to you with great frankness; I take great pride in you. I am greatly encouraged; in all our troubles my joy knows no bounds.

For when we came into Macedonia, we had no rest, but we were harassed at every turn—conflicts on the outside, fears within. But God, who comforts the downcast, comforted us by the coming of Titus, and not only by his coming but also by the comfort you had given him. He told us about your longing for me, your deep sorrow, your ardent concern for me, so that my joy was greater than ever.

Even if I caused you sorrow by my letter, I do not regret it. Though I did regret it—I see that my letter hurt you, but only for a little while— yet now I am happy, not because you were made sorry, but because your sorrow led you to repentance. For you became sorrowful as God intended and so were not harmed in any way by us. Godly sorrow brings repentance that leads to salvation and leaves no regret, but worldly sorrow brings death. See what this godly sorrow has produced in you: what earnestness, what eagerness to clear yourselves, what indignation, what alarm, what longing, what concern, what readiness to see justice done. At every point you have proved yourselves to be innocent in this matter. So even though I wrote to you, it was neither on account of the one who did the wrong nor on account of the injured party, but rather that before God you could see for yourselves how devoted to us you are. By all this we are encouraged.

In addition to our own encouragement, we were especially delighted to see how happy Titus was, because his spirit has been refreshed by all of you. I had boasted to him about you, and you have not embarrassed me. But just as everything we said to you was true, so our boasting about you to Titus has proved to be true as well. And his affection for you is all the greater when he remembers that you were all obedient, receiving him with fear and trembling. I am glad I can have complete confidence in you.

And now, brothers and sisters, we want you to know about the grace that God has given the

Macedonian churches. In the midst of a very severe trial, their overflowing joy and their extreme poverty welled up in rich generosity. For I testify that they gave as much as they were able, and even beyond their ability. Entirely on their own, they urgently pleaded with us for the privilege of sharing in this service to the Lord's people. And they exceeded our expectations: They gave themselves first of all to the Lord, and then by the will of God also to us. So we urged Titus, just as he had earlier made a beginning, to bring also to completion this act of grace on your part. But since you excel in everything—in faith, in speech, in knowledge, in complete earnestness and in the love we have kindled in you—see that you also excel in this grace of giving.

I am not commanding you, but I want to test the sincerity of your love by comparing it with the earnestness of others. For you know the grace of our Lord Jesus Christ, that though he was rich, yet for your sake he became poor, so that you through his poverty might become rich.

And here is my judgment about what is best for you in this matter. Last year you were the first not only to give but also to have the desire to do so. Now finish the work, so that your eager willingness to do it may be matched by your completion of it, according to your means. For if the willingness is there, the gift is acceptable according to what one has, not according to what one does not have.

Our desire is not that others might be relieved while you are hard pressed, but that there might be equality. At the present time your plenty will supply what they need, so that in turn their plenty will supply what you need. The goal is equality, as it is written: "The one who gathered much did not have too much, and the one who gathered little did not have too little."

Thanks be to God, who put into the heart of Titus the same concern I have for you. For Titus not only welcomed our appeal, but he is coming to you with much enthusiasm and on his own initiative. And we are sending along with him the brother who is praised by all the churches for his service to the gospel. What is more, he was chosen by the churches to accompany us as we carry the offering, which we administer in order to honor the Lord himself and to show our eagerness to help. We want to avoid any criticism of the way we administer this liberal gift. For we are taking pains to do what is right, not only in the eyes of the Lord but also in the eyes of man.

In addition, we are sending with them our brother who has often proved to us in many ways that he is zealous, and now even more so because of his great confidence in you. As for Titus, he is my partner and co-worker among you; as for our brothers, they are representatives of the churches and an honor to Christ. Therefore show these men the proof of your love and the reason for our pride in you, so that the churches can see it.

There is no need for me to write to you about this service to the Lord's people. For I know your eagerness to help, and I have been boasting about it to the Macedonians, telling them that since last year you in Achaia were ready to give; and your enthusiasm has stirred most of them to action. But I am sending the brothers in order that our boasting about you in this matter should not prove hollow, but that you may be ready, as I said you would be. For if any Macedonians come with me and find you unprepared, we—not to say anything about you—would be ashamed of having been so confident. So I thought it necessary to urge the brothers to visit you in advance and finish the arrangements for the generous gift you had promised. Then it will be ready as a generous gift, not as one grudgingly given.

Remember this: Whoever sows sparingly will also reap sparingly, and whoever sows generously will also reap generously. Each of you should give what you have decided in your heart to give, not reluctantly or under compulsion, for God loves a cheerful giver. And God is able to bless you abundantly, so that in all things at all times, having all that you need, you will abound in every good work. As it is written:

"They have freely scattered their gifts to the poor; their righteousness endures forever."

Now he who supplies seed to the sower and bread for food will also supply and increase your store of seed and will enlarge the harvest of your righteousness. You will be enriched in every way so that you can be generous on every occasion, and through us your generosity will result in thanksgiving to God.

This service that you perform is not only supplying the needs of the Lord's people but is also overflowing in many expressions of thanks to God. Because of the service by which you have proved yourselves, others will praise God for the obedience that accompanies your confession of the gospel of Christ, and for your generosity in sharing with them and with everyone else. And in their prayers for you their hearts will go out to you, because of the surpassing grace God has given you. Thanks be to God for his indescribable gift!

By the humility and gentleness of Christ, I appeal to you—I, Paul, who am "timid" when face to face with you, but "bold" toward you when away! I beg you that when I come I may not have to be as bold as I expect to be toward some people who think that we live by the standards of this world. For though we live in the world, we do not wage war as the world does. The weapons we fight with are not the weapons of the world. On the contrary, they have divine power to demolish strongholds. We demolish arguments and every pretension that sets itself up against the knowledge of God, and we take captive every thought to make it obedient to Christ. And we will be ready to punish every act of disobedience, once your obedience is complete.

You are judging by appearances. If anyone is confident that they belong to Christ, they should consider again that we belong to Christ just as much as they do. So even if I boast somewhat freely about the authority the Lord gave us for building you up rather than tearing you down, I will not be ashamed of it. I do not want to seem to be trying to frighten you with my letters. For some say, "His letters are weighty and forceful, but in person he is unimpressive and his speaking amounts to nothing." Such people should realize that what we are in our letters when we are absent, we will be in our actions when we are present.

We do not dare to classify or compare ourselves with some who commend themselves. When they measure themselves by themselves and compare themselves with themselves, they are not wise. We, however, will not boast beyond proper limits, but will confine our boasting to the sphere of service God himself has assigned to us, a sphere that also includes you. We are not going too far in our boasting, as would be the case if we had not come to you, for we did get as far as you with the gospel of Christ. Neither do we go beyond our limits by boasting of work done by others. Our hope is that, as your faith continues to grow, our sphere of activity among you will greatly expand, so that we can preach the gospel in the regions beyond you. For we do not want to boast about work already done in someone else's territory. But, "Let the one who boasts boast in the Lord." For it is not the one who commends himself who is approved, but the one whom the Lord commends.

I hope you will put up with me in a little foolishness. Yes, please put up with me! I am jealous for you with a godly jealousy. I promised you to one husband, to Christ, so that I might present you as a pure virgin to him. But I am afraid that just as Eve was deceived by the serpent's cunning, your minds may somehow be led astray from your sincere and pure devotion to Christ. For if someone comes to you and preaches a Jesus other than the Jesus we preached, or if you receive a different spirit from the Spirit you received, or a different gospel from the one you accepted, you put up with it easily enough.

I do not think I am in the least inferior to those "super-apostles." I may indeed be untrained as a speaker, but I do have knowledge. We have made this perfectly clear to you in every way. Was it a sin for me to lower myself in order to elevate you by preaching the gospel of God to you free of charge? I robbed other churches by receiving support from them so as to serve you. And when I was with you and needed something, I was not a burden to anyone, for the brothers who came from Macedonia supplied what I needed. I have kept myself from being a burden to you in any way, and will continue to do so. As surely as the truth of Christ is in me, nobody in the regions of Achaia will stop this boasting of mine. Why? Because I do not love you? God knows I do!

And I will keep on doing what I am doing in order to cut the ground from under those who want an opportunity to be considered equal with us in the things they boast about. For such people are false apostles, deceitful workers, masquerading as apostles of Christ. And no wonder, for Satan himself masquerades as an angel of light. It is not surprising, then, if his servants also masquerade as servants of righteousness. Their end will be what their actions deserve.

I repeat: Let no one take me for a fool. But if you do, then tolerate me just as you would a fool, so that I may do a little boasting. In this self-confident boasting I am not talking as the Lord would, but as a fool. Since many are boasting in the way the world does, I too will boast. You gladly put up with fools since you are so wise! In fact, you even put up with anyone who enslaves you or exploits you or takes advantage of you or puts on airs or slaps you in the face. To my shame I admit that we were too weak for that!

Whatever anyone else dares to boast about—I am speaking as a fool—I also dare to boast about. Are they Hebrews? So am I. Are they Israelites? So am I. Are they Abraham's descendants? So am I. Are they servants of Christ? (I am out of my mind to talk like this.) I am more. I have worked much harder, been in prison more frequently, been flogged more severely, and been exposed to death again and again. Five times I received from the Jews the forty lashes minus one. Three times I was beaten with rods, once I was pelted with stones, three times I was shipwrecked, I spent a night and a day in the open sea, I have been constantly on the move. I have been in danger from rivers, in danger from bandits, in danger from my fellow Jews, in danger from Gentiles; in danger in the city, in danger in the country, in danger at sea; and in danger from false believers. I have labored and toiled and have often gone without sleep; I have known hunger and thirst and have often gone without food; I have been cold and naked. Besides everything else, I face daily the pressure of my concern for all the churches. Who is weak, and I do not feel weak? Who is led into sin, and I do not inwardly burn?

If I must boast, I will boast of the things that show my weakness. The God and Father of the Lord Jesus, who is to be praised forever, knows that I am not lying. In Damascus the governor under King Aretas had the city of the Damascenes guarded in order to arrest me. But I was lowered in a basket from a window in the wall and slipped through his hands.

I must go on boasting. Although there is nothing to be gained, I will go on to visions and revelations from the Lord. I know a man in Christ who fourteen years ago was caught up to the third heaven. Whether it was in the body or out of the body I do not know—God knows. And I know that this man—whether in the body or apart from the body I do not know, but God knows— was caught up to paradise and heard inexpressible things, things that no one is permitted to tell. I will boast about a man like that, but I will not boast about myself, except about my weaknesses. Even if I should choose to boast, I would not be a fool, because I would be speaking the truth. But I refrain, so no one will think more of me than is warranted by what I do or say, or because of these surpassingly great revelations. Therefore, in order to keep me from becoming conceited, I was given a thorn in my flesh, a messenger of Satan, to torment me. Three times I pleaded with the Lord to take it away from me. But he said to me, "My grace is sufficient for you, for my power is made perfect in weakness." Therefore I will boast all the more gladly about my weaknesses, so that Christ's power may rest on me. That is why, for Christ's sake, I delight in weaknesses, in insults, in hardships, in persecutions, in difficulties. For when I am weak, then I am strong.

I have made a fool of myself, but you drove me to it. I ought to have been commended by you, for I am not in the least inferior to the "super-apostles," even though I am nothing. I persevered in demonstrating among you the marks of a true apostle, including signs, wonders and miracles. How were you inferior to the other churches, except that I was never a burden to you? Forgive me this wrong!

Now I am ready to visit you for the third time, and I will not be a burden to you, because what I want is not your possessions but you. After all, children should not have to save up for their parents, but parents for their children. So I will very gladly spend for you everything I have and expend myself as well. If I love you more, will you love me less? Be that as it may, I have not been a burden to you. Yet, crafty fellow that I am, I caught you by trickery! Did I exploit you through any of the men I sent to you? I urged Titus to go to you and I sent our brother with him. Titus did not exploit you, did he? Did we not walk in the same footsteps by the same Spirit?

Have you been thinking all along that we have been defending ourselves to you? We have been speaking in the sight of God as those in Christ; and everything we do, dear friends, is for your strengthening. For I am afraid that when I come I may not find you as I want you to be, and you may not find me as you want me to be. I fear that there may be discord, jealousy, fits of rage, selfish ambition, slander, gossip, arrogance and disorder. I am afraid that when I come again my God will humble me before you, and I will be grieved over many who have sinned earlier and have not repented of the impurity, sexual sin and debauchery in which they have indulged.

This will be my third visit to you. "Every matter must be established by the testimony of two or three witnesses." I already gave you a warning when I was with you the second time. I now repeat it while absent: On my return I will not spare those who sinned earlier or any of the others, since you are demanding proof that Christ is speaking through me. He is not weak in dealing with you, but is powerful among you. For to be sure, he was crucified in weakness, yet he lives by God's power. Likewise, we are weak in him, yet by God's power we will live with him in our dealing with you.

Examine yourselves to see whether you are in the faith; test yourselves. Do you not realize that Christ Jesus is in you—unless, of course, you fail the test? And I trust that you will discover that we have not failed the test. Now we pray to God that you will not do anything wrong—not so that people will see that we have stood the test but so that you will do what is right even though we may seem to have failed. For we cannot do anything against the truth, but only for the truth. We are glad whenever we are weak but you are strong; and our prayer is that you may be fully restored. This is why I write these things when I am absent, that when I come I may not have to be harsh in my use of authority—the authority the Lord gave me for building you up, not for tearing you down.

Finally, brothers and sisters, rejoice! Strive for full restoration, encourage one another, be of one mind, live in peace. And the God of love and peace will be with you.

Greet one another with a holy kiss. All God's people here send their greetings.

May the grace of the Lord Jesus Christ, and the love of God, and the fellowship of the Holy Spirit be with you all.

INTRODUCTION

PODCAST LISTENER GUIDE

> **Recommended:** Listen to the podcast "The Call to Dependent Living" as an introduction to the whole study. Use the following listener guide.

The Call to Dependent Living

The main emphasis of the book of 2 Corinthians is that we, as believers in Christ, should live our lives dependent on Him all the time in our strengths and in our weaknesses.

ABOUT PAUL

- The Corinthians knew Paul as being well-educated, a tent-making craftsman, determined, bold, convinced of the truth of Christ, and very committed to Jesus' calling on his life. He was a gifted teacher and loved God's people almost as much as he loved God Himself.

- Five years had passed from the time of the beginning of the church in Corinth until the time of Paul writing this letter. Based upon scriptural references, second Corinthians is Paul's fourth letter to the church at Corinth. The Holy Spirit only preserved two for us—First and Second Corinthians.

- To gain perspective on Paul's relationship with the Corinthians, think back over the last five years of your relationship with a group of people that don't live with you but you visit occasionally and with whom you may have a rough relationship. What was that relationship like five years ago? What is it like now? What have your visits with them been like? How did you hear about them between visits? What makes the relationship rough?

THE TRUTH ABOUT BECOMING GOD-DEPENDENT IN OUR MESSY LIVES

- This letter we know as 2 Corinthians is one of Paul's most personal letters. It is not a "sermon" like Romans or Ephesians that can be easily outlined. It is a messy letter, just like most personal letters. It is full of personal feelings and experiences interspersed between some terrific teaching. It is like life—messy—because people are messy, relationships are messy, circumstances are messy, and community within the church is messy.

- God wants for us women to be God-dependent women. Not "independent except for when we need Him." But we are to be God-dependent. All. The. Time.

- But being God-dependent all the time is so radically different from what our culture teaches. If you have been reared in western culture, this is contrary to what you have been taught most of your life. It is opposite of self-reliance as the way to be a strong, effective woman.

- Are we as Christian women supposed to stay like babies not doing anything for ourselves? No! We are supposed to grow and mature in our thinking and behavior.

- Are we as Christian women supposed to just lie back and let anything happen to us? No! That is not what it means. The New Testament teaches Christians to be wise and proactive in our dealings with everyone—whether in the church or outside of it—for our own good as well as for the good of others.

- Are we not supposed to use our skills, talents, advantages, and opportunities to be the best women we can be? No! That is not what it means. God wants us to give back to Him all our skills, talents, advantages, and opportunities He has given to us and use them for His glory. That involves following His leading and guidance. Sometimes, our strength can be our greatest hindrance. We tend to rely on that rather than on God. So, relying on God means submitting your strengths and your weaknesses to Him for His purposes in your life.

DEPENDENT LIVING IS THE KEY TO BECOMING A GOD-DEPENDENT WOMAN

Human parents raise their children to be less dependent on them and more independent of them. But God raises His children to be less independent and more dependent on Him.

- The key to being a God-dependent woman is what can be described as dependent living. Whatever He brings into our lives that makes us more dependent upon Him is good for us.

- Dependent living is not weakness. It is being stronger and having more influence, success, and satisfaction than you could ever have through your own efforts—as brilliant and self-sufficient as you think you are or as weak and messed up as you think you are and everywhere in-between.

- Through this 11-week study of 2 Corinthians, we will learn how to make plans for our lives and rely on the Lord with how to proceed. We will learn how to educate our minds and rely on the Lord to use that knowledge to glorify Him. We will learn how to make money and rely on the Lord to show us how to use it wisely. We learn how to do this as we act in obedience to the Word of God, depend on Jesus Christ for the power to do so, and trust Him with the results. This "dependent living" will make us stronger and more effective in life than we could ever be on our own.

- There is great value for every woman to study this messy, hard to read letter we call Second Corinthians—parent, teacher, mentor to teens and young adults, and every woman wanting a closer relationship with Christ.

- You can have confidence in what the Lord Jesus Christ will do in your life so that you will want to depend on Him more than on yourself. As you submit to Him, our God will transform you into a God-dependent woman who lives dependently on Him in weakness and in strength. Nothing could be better!

Let Jesus satisfy your heart with confidence that you can depend on Him. Then, live each day as a God-dependent woman!

1: The God on Whom We Can Rely

2 Corinthians 1:1-11

But this happened that we might not rely on ourselves but on God, who raises the dead. (2 Corinthians 1:9b, Memory Verse #1)

DAY ONE STUDY

The ABCs of 2nd Corinthians—Author, Background, and Context

Like any book you read, it always helps to know a bit about the author, the background setting for the story (i.e., past, present, future), and where the book fits into a series (That is the context). The same is true of Bible books.

AUTHOR

Paul identifies himself as the author of this letter written to the church at Corinth. Paul, whose Hebrew name was Saul, was born in Tarsus, a major Roman city on the coast of southeast Asia Minor. Tarsus was the center for the tent making industry. Paul was trained in that craft as his occupation (his primary paying profession). As a Jewish Pharisee from the tribe of Benjamin, Paul was educated at the feet of Gamaliel, a well-respected rabbi of the day. Paul was an ardent persecutor of the early church until his life-changing conversion to Christianity

After believing in Jesus Christ as his Savior, God called Paul to take the gospel to the Gentiles (non-Jews). This was an amazing about-face for a committed Pharisee like Paul who ordinarily would have nothing to do with Gentiles. Paul wrote 13 letters that are included in the New Testament. Tradition has it that Paul was beheaded shortly after he wrote 2nd Timothy in 67 AD. *(The above information comes from Acts 8:3; 9:1-31; 22:3-5; 26:9-11; and Galatians 1:11-24.)*

BACKGROUND

Around 44 B.C., Julius Caesar rebuilt Corinth from a pile of rubble into a great Roman capital city. So, it was relatively young by the time of Paul without aristocracy, traditions, or well-established citizens. As a Roman colony and the capital of the province of Achaia, the people who called Corinth home were mostly retired Roman soldiers, merchants (many of whom were Jews) and other immigrants from the East. Corinth's strategic location brought commerce and all that goes with it: wealth, a steady stream of travelers and merchants, and vice (including prostitution as part of the worship of their local gods and goddesses). Corinthians had a reputation for wealth and sensuality.

As we read Acts and Paul's letters to the Corinthians, we can piece together a lot of the background information for this letter. On his second missionary journey, Paul spent a year and a half in Corinth (A.D. 51-52). Then, Paul went to Ephesus on his third missionary journey and made that city his base of operations for almost three years (A.D. 53-56). There he heard disturbing news about immorality in the Corinthian church. So, he wrote a letter urging the believers not to tolerate such conduct in their midst. Paul referred to this previous letter in 1 Corinthians 5:9. It has not been preserved.

After this, Paul heard from "Chloe's people" that factions had developed in the church. He also received a letter from the church in Corinth requesting his guidance on certain matters. Those who carried this letter also reported other disturbing conditions in the church. These factors led Paul to compose another letter, the one we call "1 Corinthians," in which he dealt with the questions and problems, promised to visit them soon, and said he was sending Timothy to Corinth. Paul sent this letter from Ephesus by trusted messengers in the late winter or early spring of A.D. 55.

There was internal strife in the Corinthian church. But the larger problem seems to have been that some in the community were leading the church into a view of things that was contrary to that which Paul taught them. This resulted in a questioning of Paul's authority and his gospel.

While the letter we know as "1 Corinthians" did not dispel the problems in the church at Corinth completely, it resolved some of them. Yet, opposition to the Apostle Paul persisted. Paul's critics continued to speak out against him in the church, claiming equal authority with Paul and questioning whether Paul was really an apostle. The Christians in Corinth didn't argue with what he had written; they simply denied his right to tell them what to do.

News of continuing problems in Corinth reached Paul in Ephesus so he made a brief visit to Corinth. What he called "a painful visit," his efforts to resolve the conflicts proved unsuccessful. He then returned to Ephesus and sent a "severe letter" from Ephesus carried by Titus and another unnamed believer. This letter has not been preserved.

While waiting to receive the report back from Titus' visit, persecution made Paul leave Ephesus earlier than he had anticipated. He found an open door for the gospel to the north in Troas. Eager to meet Titus, who was taking the land route from Corinth back to Ephesus, Paul moved west into Macedonia. There Titus met him and gave him an encouraging report. Most of the church had responded to Paul's directives, and the church had disciplined the troublemakers. Unfortunately, some in the congregation still refused to acknowledge Paul's authority over them.

Paul wrote what we know as "2 Corinthians" from Macedonia (Philippi, Thessalonica, or Berea) probably in the fall or winter of A.D. 56. (*The above information adapted from Dr. Constable's Notes on 1 Corinthians and 2 Corinthians, 2018 Editions*)

CONTEXT

Though found in our New Testaments after the book of Romans, Paul wrote 1 Corinthians (from Ephesus) and 2 Corinthians (from Macedonia) before he wrote Romans during his stay in Corinth.

> **Historical Insight:** Trying to piece together this section of Paul's life and ministry is like assembling a picture puzzle without the box-top. The big pieces are easy, but the small ones drive you crazy! (Steve Hixon, *The New Covenant Lifestyle*, p. 3)

Here is a possible timeline:

Paul's founding visit	Paul's first letter	The Corinthians' letter to Paul	*First Corinthians*	The "painful visit"	Paul's "severe letter"	Titus brings news	*Second Corinthians*	Paul's next visit
				2 Cor. 2:1	2 Cor. 2:4	2 Cor. 2:13; 7:5-7	2 Cor. 2:4	Acts 20:3
Spring 51	1 Cor. 5:9	1 Cor. 1:11; 7:1; 16:17	**Spring 55**	**Summer/Fall 55**			**Fall 56**	**Winter 56/57**

1. What grabbed your attention as you read the ABC's of the book of 2 Corinthians?

The God-Dependent Woman and Dependent Living

This letter, 2 Corinthians, is considered one of Paul's most personal letters. It is not a "sermon" like Romans or Ephesians that can be easily outlined. It is a messy letter, just like most personal letters. It is full of personal feelings and experiences interspersed between some terrific teaching. It is like life—messy—because people are messy, relationships are messy, circumstances are messy, and community within the church is messy.

> The majority of New Testament writings exist because the early church was messy ... Emerging from the mess is the fingerprint of God writing the hope of the gospel and the story of redemption. (Heather Zempel, *Community Is Messy*, pages 24, 26-27)

In the midst of our messy lives, God wants us to learn to rely on Him more than on ourselves. If you have been reared in western culture, this is contrary to what you have been taught most of your life. To compensate for poor teaching in the past, women are taught from girlhood to "stand on your own two feet" and "you don't need anyone to be successful." So, what does this relying on God look like?

Are we as Christians supposed to stay like babies not doing anything for ourselves? Does it mean we are supposed to just lie back and let anything happen to us? Does it mean we aren't supposed to use our skills, talents, advantages, and opportunities to be the best we can be? No! That is not what it means.

We are supposed to grow and mature in our thinking and behavior. God wants us to give to Him all our skills, talents, advantages, and opportunities and use them for His glory. That involves following His leading and guidance. It means submitting our strengths and our weaknesses to Him for His purpose in our lives.

Here is the key to this: Human parents raise their children to be less dependent on them and more independent. But God raises His children to be *less independent* and **more dependent on Him.** Whatever He brings into our lives that makes us more dependent upon Him is good for us. The key to being a God-dependent woman is **dependent living**.

Throughout 2 Corinthians, we will see examples of dependent living. Paul makes plans and submits them to God to be changed. We will see him demonstrating his authority as a leader and submitting that to God. He asks for healing and submits to God's answer. And Paul talks about preaching the gospel in one city while his heart wants to be in another city, waiting for God to say "go." That is dependent living.

Dependent living is not weakness. It is being stronger and having more influence, success, and satisfaction than we could ever have through our own efforts—as brilliant and self-sufficient as we think we are or as weak and messed up as we think we are and everywhere in-between.

Through this 11-week study of 2 Corinthians, we will learn how to make plans for our lives and rely on the Lord with how to proceed. We will learn how to educate our minds and rely on the Lord to use that knowledge to glorify Him. We will learn how to make money and rely on the Lord to show us how to use it wisely. We learn how to do this as we act in obedience to the Word of God, depend on Jesus Christ for the power to do so, and trust Him with the results. This "dependent living" will make us stronger and more effective in life than we could ever be on our own.

As a reminder, you will see this main idea at the end of each lesson:

As His child, God transforms your life by teaching you to live dependently on Him in weakness and in strength.

The following verses describe or relate to dependent living. To help you learn about living dependently on the Lord, we recommend you memorize the verses listed below. I have included the NIV version of each, but you can use any translation. Write them on cards and place them where you will see and review them.

> *But this happened that we might not rely on ourselves but on God, who raises the dead. (2 Corinthians 1:9b)*
>
> *But we have this treasure in jars of clay to show that this all-surpassing power is from God and not from us. (2 Corinthians 4:7)*
>
> *But he said to me, "My grace is sufficient for you, for my power is made perfect in weakness." Therefore I will boast all the more gladly about my weaknesses, so that Christ's power may rest on me. That is why, for Christ's sake, I delight in weaknesses, in insults, in hardships, in persecutions, in difficulties. For when I am weak, then I am strong. (2 Corinthians 12:9-10)*

2. What questions do you have about "dependent living" that you hope to have answered through this study?

DAY TWO STUDY

This day will take a little longer than most because we ask you to read through the entire letter of 2 Corinthians. Reading through the whole letter is the best way to see the entire message and get the "big picture" before we divide it into smaller pieces to enjoy it more slowly.

For your convenience, the letter of 2 Corinthians is provided for you in the pages before this lesson. Or you can read it in your own Bible.

Read the letter called "2 Corinthians" as it was intended ... a letter from one dear friend to another. Read it at one sitting. It will take about 40 minutes. Consider the following questions as you read. Ready? Go!

3. What do you remember the most from your reading of this entire letter? What topics, situations, or teachings does Paul include in his letter that particularly interest you?

Ask God to show you answers to your questions and what He wants you to learn through this study of 2 Corinthians.

LESSON ONE

DAY THREE STUDY—GET THE BIG PICTURE

Let's start digging into this wonderful letter from God to us. For every lesson, we will begin with reading the whole passage to get the big picture before we study the verses more closely.

Ask the Lord Jesus to teach you through His Word. (✱This is a dependent living choice.)

Read the Bible passage below (NIV). Use your own method (colored pencils, lines, shapes) to mark 1) anything that grabs your attention and 2) words you want to understand. Feel free to develop your own method of marking up a passage. ☺ Put a star ✱ next to anything you think relates to dependent living. I have shown you one examples (v. 4).

1 Paul, an apostle of Christ Jesus by the will of God, and Timothy our brother,

To the church of God in Corinth, together with all his holy people throughout Achaia:

2 Grace and peace to you from God our Father and the Lord Jesus Christ.

3 Praise be to the God and Father of our Lord Jesus Christ, the Father of compassion and the God of all comfort, 4 who comforts us in all our troubles, so that we can comfort those in any trouble with the comfort we ourselves receive from God✱. 5 For just as we share abundantly in the sufferings of Christ, so also our comfort abounds through Christ. 6 If we are distressed, it is for your comfort and salvation; if we are comforted, it is for your comfort, which produces in you patient endurance of the same sufferings we suffer. 7 And our hope for you is firm, because we know that just as you share in our sufferings, so also you share in our comfort.

8 We do not want you to be uninformed, brothers and sisters, about the troubles we experienced in the province of Asia. We were under great pressure, far beyond our ability to endure, so that we despaired of life itself. 9 Indeed, we felt we had received the sentence of death. But this happened that we might not rely on ourselves but on God, who raises the dead. 10 He has delivered us from such a deadly peril, and he will deliver us again. On him we have set our hope that he will continue to deliver us, 11 as you help us by your prayers. Then many will give thanks on our behalf for the gracious favor granted us in answer to the prayers of many.

4. What grabbed your attention from this passage?

   - vv. 1-2

   - vv. 3-7

   - vv. 8-11

5. What verses or specific words do you want to understand better?

THE GOD-DEPENDENT WOMAN

6. What verses illustrate or help you understand what dependent living on God looks like?

   Example: We receive comfort from God for ourselves and to comfort others. (v. 4)

What does the Bible say? *(This is the "Observation" step in the process of Bible Study.)*

7. Focus on vv. 1-2. This is called the "salutation." In ancient letters, the salutation included both the letter writer and the recipient's name. Email today emulates this in some ways.

   The letter is from Paul. He is what?

   Who is with Paul?

   Who are the recipients?

   How does Paul begin his greeting (v. 2)?

   > **Historical Insight:** Paul intended that the Corinthian Christians would read this epistle in the church, but he also wanted all the Christians in the province of Achaia to read it. We know that at this time there was another church a few miles away in Cenchrea (Romans 16:1), and perhaps one in nearby Athens (Acts 17:34). (*Dr. Constable's Notes on 2 Corinthians 2017 Edition*, p. 10)

What does it mean? *(This is the "Interpretation" step in the process of Bible Study.)*

8. Read 1 Corinthians 1:26. What does Paul say about the Corinthians that might help you to identify with them?

9. Read the following verses to compare Paul's salutations in other letters. Galatians 1:1-3 (Paul's first letter); 1 Corinthians 1:1-3 (written before 2 Corinthians); Romans 1:1, 7-8 (written after 2 Corinthians) and Ephesians 1:1-2 (one of Paul's last letters). What is consistently the same?

LESSON ONE

Focus on the Meaning: "Grace" was a common Greek salutation that meant "greetings" or "rejoice." The Jews said "shalom" to each other, meaning "peace and prosperity." Paul used both words when he greeted the recipients of his epistles. For the Christian, these terms took on a deeper meaning. God has chosen to set His love upon the believer in Christ (grace) resulting in something that the world cannot give (peace).

What application will you make? *(This is the "Application" step in the process of Bible Study.)*

10. Being confident in the authenticity of what you read in the Bible is important to your faith. How would the consistency you found in the previous question help to prove the authenticity of those letters? By the way, skeptics concede that Paul wrote 2 Corinthians. No argument about it.

Day Four Study

Read 2 Corinthians 1:3-11. Ask the Lord Jesus to teach you through His Word.

What does the Bible say?

11. Answer these questions from the text.

    Praise be to _____,

    the Father of _____ and the God of

    _____ (v. 3).

    When God comforts us, what can we do (v. 4)?

    We share abundantly in what two things of Christ (v. 5)?

    What does sharing someone else's sufferings and comfort from God produce in us (v. 6)?

    Paul and his friends suffered hardships in Asia. How did they feel during that time (vv. 8-9)?

    What purpose did they see in their sufferings (v. 9)?

    What did God do that fed their hope (v. 10)?

Who will benefit from the prayers of the Corinthians (v. 11)?

Did anything else grab your attention?

What does it mean?

12. Paul describes God as "the Father of compassion" (v. 3) and "the God of **all** comfort," the one to whom we should go first in our troubles. Compassion means to not just feel sympathy for someone's pain but to do something to alleviate it. Paul equates this with receiving "comfort" from God.

    - Define the verb "comfort."

    - How does our God of compassion comfort us? Consider all the ways that He uses to do so.

    Scriptural Insight: God is not detached, cold, and distant. He knows, understands, empathizes with, and responds to the pain in our lives with compassion. This is beautifully illustrated in the life of Jesus (see Mark 6:34). Jesus promised in John 14:16 that He send the Holy Spirit to be our comforter (Gr. parakletos, "to come alongside, called to one's aid"). *Comfort* translates a related Greek word meaning "a calling near, esp. for help"). Our God comes alongside us to give us Himself and His strength to face the trouble.

13. What did Paul mean when he said we share abundantly in the sufferings of Christ (v. 5)? Think of the human sufferings that we share with Jesus.

14. Paul wrote this letter after experiencing severe trials in Ephesus (vv. 8-9). Read Acts 19:23-41 and 1 Corinthians 15:32. What did he experience?

LESSON ONE

Although the context of Paul's "sufferings" may be persecution, the principle applies to any troubles experienced by humans. Jesus experienced them all except those brought on by personal sinfulness since He was sinless. But He understands our need for comfort even then.

15. Paul admitted weakness. Being a mature Christian doesn't exempt you from fear, struggle, doubt, stress and suffering. Paul viewed those experiences as opportunities for learning to rely on God more than oneself (v. 9).

    - What does it mean to rely on or trust someone?

    - What choices must you make to rely on God more than on yourself?

16. When you have trouble in your life, someone might tell you this, "God doesn't give you more than you can handle." Based upon what you read in vv. 8-9, why is that a false teaching?

    Think About It: God allows painful things to happen to His children. He puts us in situations where it's beyond our ability. We are still capable of sinning. We can't fully trust ourselves. He gives us more than we can handle on our own so we are forced to trust in Him.

17. Read 1 Corinthians 10:13. What does God promise regarding any temptation to sin that you face at any time? How is this also teaching you to rely on God more than yourself?

    From the Greek: "Gracious favor" NIV / "blessing" ESV (2 Corinthians 1:11) comes from the Greek word *charisma* meaning "a favor with which one receives without any merit of his own." This undeserved gift of divine grace towards us stems from God's love for us. God chooses to give it because of His love so that men and women can become acceptable to Him. Grace is summed up in the name, person, and work of the Lord Jesus Christ. We receive this favor or acceptance from God as a free gift through faith. God's grace is all-sufficient, and our weakness is precisely the opportunity for His power to be displayed.

THE GOD-DEPENDENT WOMAN

Did you see something else in this passage that you wanted to study more? This is where you would use an online tool or app (blueletterbible.org or "Blue Letter Bible app" is especially helpful) to find *cross references* (verses with similar content to what you are studying) and meanings of the *original Greek words or phrases* used (usually called "interlinear"). You can also look at any verse in *various Bible translations* to help with understanding what it is saying. These tools help you get a clearer picture of the meaning of a passage after you have studied if for yourself. You will have the opportunity to add your own study at the end of every **What does it mean?** section.

18. What else did you learn as you studied 2 Corinthians 1:3-11?

What application will you make?

19. If you consider that God's purpose in allowing troubles in your life is to lead you to rely on Him more than yourself (v. 9):

    - How do you recognize when you are relying on yourself more than on God?

    - How resistant are you to giving up control? Do you want to learn to give up control?

    - What would be the benefits of relying on God more than on yourself?

    Think About It: Suffering drives us to dependence on God. We set our hope on Him more than ourselves. We see His love and grace given to us. We give thanks.

20. Read vv. 4, 6-7, 11 again. God has purpose even for our pain. Read v. 4 in "The Message" translation. In what ways have your struggles led to helping someone else? Give an example from a real-life relationship.

LESSON ONE

21. In what other ways can you apply this lesson to your life?

22. Review the passage for this lesson in "Day One Study." Add reasons why God wants us to depend on Him more than on ourselves to the chart below. I have given a few prompts.

Verse(s)	Reasons why God wants us to depend on Him more than on ourselves
v. 4	We receive comfort from God for ourselves and to comfort others.
v. 9	He is more powerful than we are.
v. 10	
v. 11	

Think About It: Every daily lesson in this study begins and ends with prayer. Prayer is conversation with Someone who loves you dearly. It is not about magic words or formulas. God speaks to you through His word. You may respond to Him about anything and ask Him to make His word true in your life. Lack of prayer is often a sign of self-sufficiency rather than dependent living.

Respond to the Lord about what He has shown you today.

As His child, God transforms your life by teaching you to live dependently on Him in weakness and in strength.

> **Recommended:** Listen to the podcast "Confidence in God Encourages Dependence on Him" to reinforce what you have learned. Use the following listener guide.

Confidence in God Encourages Dependence on Him

PRAISE GOD FOR HIS COMFORT

- Paul describes God as "the Father of compassion" (v. 3) and "the God of **all** comfort," the one to whom we should go first in our troubles. Compassion means to not just feel sympathy for someone's pain but to do something to alleviate it. To comfort means "to give strength, to console, and to aid." That is what God does for us. He gives us strength to sustain us through the pain of life on earth.

- The most wonderful thing is knowing that our Lord Jesus Christ experienced this fallen world just like we do. He totally understands every suffering you and I experience. Because He was 100% human as well as 100% God, He knows exactly how to comfort us and sustain us through our pain.

- Most of the time God uses His Word to comfort us. You know how some verses just jump out at you when you are needing comfort.

- God comforts us through people He sends our way. Many people have stories of how God sent someone to them to give comfort during a time of grief.

- God comforts us through the prayers of other believers. Our prayers don't change God's purposes for us (Philippians 2:13). But knowing that others are praying for us gives us strength to endure the pain. When they hear how God has answered their prayer, they receive God's comfort as well. It is partnership with God to desire His purposes to be fulfilled. And God answers our prayers out of His graciousness. *2 Corinthians 1:10-11*

- God comforts us through unexpected events.

- God comforts us from the inside through His Holy Spirit who pours out God's love on us. We can have confidence in His presence with us. We never go through pain alone.

GOD'S COMFORT DOES NOT ALWAYS MEAN DELIVERANCE FROM PAIN.

- God wants for us women to be God-dependent women. The key to being a God-dependent woman is what can be described as dependent living. It is relying on His power to get us through all of life—whether we are strong and everything is going well or whether we are in pain and weakness and in dire need of relief. Whatever God brings into our lives that makes us more dependent upon Him is good for us. That is how we learn dependent living.

- But the world and even other Christians will try to tell us that God does not want you to suffer and that we have been delivered from all suffering by our benevolent God. If you are suffering, you must have done something wrong so that God is disciplining you. Get right with God, and all your troubles will go away.

- That is not biblical! You see it throughout the book of Acts. You see it throughout all of Paul's letters. You see it throughout the other New Testament writings. God allows His children to undergo very hard things. The purpose is to teach us to trust Him with all of us, not just bits of us.

- So, every week, I am going to evaluate a popular saying that especially floats around on social media.

DOES GOD NOT GIVE YOU MORE THAN YOU CAN HANDLE?

True or False? *"God doesn't give you more than you can handle."*   **FALSE**

"We do not want you to be uninformed, brothers and sisters, about the troubles we experienced in the province of Asia. We were under great pressure, far beyond our ability to endure, so that we despaired of life itself. Indeed, we felt we had received the sentence of death. But this happened that we might not rely on ourselves but on God, who raises the dead." (2 Corinthians 1:8-9).

God gives everyone—you and me and your neighbor—more than they can handle on their own in order to drive us to Him. To rely on Him. To gain the confidence in Him so that we will depend on Him more. Life is hard, but God is good. Don't panic! Trust in the one who has the power to raise the dead.

REASONS WHY GOD WANTS US TO DEPEND ON HIM MORE THAN ON OURSELVES

In every podcast, we'll also cover some reasons from our lesson why God wants us to depend on Him more than on ourselves. From lesson one, we get these reasons.

- ✓ We receive comfort from God for ourselves and to comfort others. (1:4)
- ✓ He is more powerful than we are. (1:9)
- ✓ We can set our hope on Him to continue to deliver us. (1:10)
- ✓ God answers our prayers out of His graciousness. (1:11)

Let Jesus satisfy your heart with confidence that you can depend on Him. Then, live each day as a God-dependent woman!

LESSON TWO

2: Promises and Faithfulness

2 Corinthians 1:12-2:13

Now it is God who makes both us and you stand firm in Christ. He anointed us, set his seal of ownership on us, and put his Spirit in our hearts as a deposit, guaranteeing what is to come. (2 Corinthians 1:21-22)

The God who comforts you understands the many kinds of suffering you undergo in daily life. Although Paul wrote about the persecution he and his friends experienced that made them fear for their lives, suffering doesn't only come from persecution, from physical danger, or from outside your circle of friends. It can also come from within the circle of those whom you love the most. Misunderstandings, behavioral conflicts, and slanderous information from others can cause hurt feelings and mistrust.

Regardless of the source, suffering drives us to dependence on God. We set our hope on Him more than ourselves. We see His love and grace given to us. We trust Him to work in the situation and give thanks. That is dependent living.

Questions to consider this week:

- Have you been in a position where you were misrepresented by others and, therefore, misunderstood by someone in close relationship to you? Whom would you trust to help with reconciliation?

- As you make plans that involve others, do you submit them to the Lord for Him to change if needed even though it might cause disappointments and misunderstandings for those involved?

DAY ONE STUDY—GET THE BIG PICTURE

Ask the Lord Jesus to teach you through His Word.

Read the Bible passage below (NIV). Use your own method (colored pencils, lines, shapes) to mark 1) anything that grabs your attention, 2) words you want to understand, and 3) topics you have seen before in this letter. Draw arrows between thoughts that connect. Put a star ✱ next to anything you think relates to dependent living.

1 12 Now this is our boast: Our conscience testifies that we have conducted ourselves in the world, and especially in our relations with you, with integrity and godly sincerity. We have done so, relying not on worldly wisdom but on God's grace. 13 For we do not write you anything you cannot read or understand. And I hope that, 14 as you have understood us in part, you will come to understand fully that you can boast of us just as we will boast of you in the day of the Lord Jesus.

15 Because I was confident of this, I wanted to visit you first so that you might benefit twice. 16 I wanted to visit you on my way to Macedonia and to come back to you from Macedonia, and then to have you send me on my way to Judea. 17 Was I fickle when I intended to do this? Or do I make my plans in a worldly manner so that in the same breath I say both "Yes, yes" and "No, no"?

18 But as surely as God is faithful, our message to you is not "Yes" and "No." 19 For the Son of God, Jesus Christ, who was preached among you by us—by me and Silas and Timothy—was not "Yes" and "No," but in him it has always been "Yes." 20 For no matter how many promises God has made, they are "Yes" in Christ. And so through him the "Amen" is spoken by us to the glory of God. 21 Now it is God who makes both us and you stand firm in Christ. He anointed us, 22 set his seal of ownership on us, and put his Spirit in our hearts as a deposit, guaranteeing what is to come.

23 I call God as my witness—and I stake my life on it—that it was in order to spare you that I did not return to Corinth. 24 Not that we lord it over your faith, but we work with you for your joy, because it is by faith you stand firm.

2 So I made up my mind that I would not make another painful visit to you. 2 For if I grieve you, who is left to make me glad but you whom I have grieved? 3 I wrote as I did, so that when I came I would not be distressed by those who should have made me rejoice. I had confidence in all of you, that you would all share my joy. 4 For I wrote you out of great distress and anguish of heart and with many tears, not to grieve you but to let you know the depth of my love for you.

5 If anyone has caused grief, he has not so much grieved me as he has grieved all of you to some extent—not to put it too severely.6 The punishment inflicted on him by the majority is sufficient. 7 Now instead, you ought to forgive and comfort him, so that he will not be overwhelmed by excessive sorrow. 8 I urge you, therefore, to reaffirm your love for him. 9 Another reason I wrote you was to see if you would stand the test and be obedient in everything. 10 Anyone you forgive, I also forgive. And what I have forgiven—if there was anything to forgive—I have forgiven in the sight of Christ for your sake, 11 in order that Satan might not outwit us. For we are not unaware of his schemes.

12 Now when I went to Troas to preach the gospel of Christ and found that the Lord had opened a door for me, 13 I still had no peace of mind, because I did not find my brother Titus there. So I said goodbye to them and went on to Macedonia.

LESSON TWO

1. What grabbed your attention from these verses?
   - 1:12-14

   - 1:15-22

   - 1:23-2:13

2. What verses or specific words do you want to understand better?

3. What topics are repeated in this passage or continue an earlier discussion in this letter?

4. What verses illustrate or help you understand what dependent living on God looks like?

Respond to the Lord about what He has shown you today.

THE GOD-DEPENDENT WOMAN

DAY TWO STUDY

Read 2 Corinthians 1:12-14. Ask the Lord Jesus to teach you through His Word.

What does the Bible say?

5. As you look for the facts from the biblical text, remember that the context of Paul's words are misunderstandings between the Corinthians and himself because of what other people are saying against him.

    Paul's conscience testifies they behaved with what (v. 12)?

    ✸ But they did not rely on what (v. 12)?

    What does Paul intentionally not do (v. 13)?

    Paul hopes that they will do what (v. 14)?

    With what result (v. 14)?

    > **From the Greek:** "Boast" is based on a Greek word meaning "the act of glorying, rejoicing." As a key word in 2 Corinthians, Paul uses it 30 times in various forms. Pay attention to all the references to those who are boasting and about what they are boasting.

What does it mean?

6. From 2 Corinthians 1:12-14, summarize what you think Paul is trying to communicate to the Corinthian believers.

7. Read 1 Corinthians 2:1-5. When Paul first met the Corinthians, what examples of worldly wisdom (literally, "fleshly, humanistic") did he not use? Why?

LESSON TWO

8. What does Paul say in 2 Corinthians 1:12 to remind them about that?

> **From the Greek:** Wisdom (Gr. *sophia,* meaning "knowledge, intelligence, learning") was one of the Corinthians' buzz words. The Greeks valued wisdom. Paul used this word or variations of it 15 times in 1 Corinthians plus 2 Corinthians 1:12.

9. What else did you learn as you studied 2 Corinthians 1:12-14?

What application will you make?

Being misrepresented by someone and, therefore, misunderstood is very painful. Paul basically tells the Corinthians, "Look at my behavior. I am single-minded and sincere. It is the truth. Please trust me. Then, we can be proud of each other's faith."

10. Have you been in a similar relationship where you were misrepresented and misunderstood? What have you learned from today's study that you could apply to your situation?

11. In what other ways can you apply this lesson to your life?

Respond to the Lord about what He has shown you today.

THE GOD-DEPENDENT WOMAN

Day Three Study

Read 2 Corinthians 1:15-22. Ask the Lord Jesus to teach you through His Word.

What does the Bible say?

12. Answer the following questions based on what is written in the biblical text.

    Since Paul was confident the Corinthians would understand the truth, what was his plan for visiting them (vv. 15-16)?

    What seems to be the accusation against Paul (v. 17)?

    Referring back to v. 12, what does Paul declare in v. 18 ("yes" and "no" refers to fickleness)?

    Whom does he call upon as his witness and example to follow (vv. 19-20)?

    Through whom is Paul's "amen / may it be fulfilled" spoken (v. 20)?

    For what purpose (v. 20)?

    According to v. 21, God does what for us?

    According to v. 22, God does what for us?

    Did anything else grab your attention?

> **Scriptural Insight:** Verse 15 can cause some confusion depending on your Bible translation. "Second experience of grace (ESV)" / "benefit twice (NIV)" comes from the Greek word *charis*, meaning gift, grace, blessing, joy, or benefit. Paul used this word in the context of his visits, not any kind of salvation or spiritual experience. He hoped that his visiting them twice would be a double blessing for them.

LESSON TWO

What does it mean?

Read Acts 19:21-22. Paul was in Ephesus when he made his initial travel plans. To understand where he was and where he was planning to go, find Ephesus, Macedonia, Corinth, and Judea on the map at right.

13. ✱ Paul made plans but left them in the Lord's hands. On what was He relying to lead him to visit Corinth? See also Acts 18:21 and James 4:13-15 for insight.

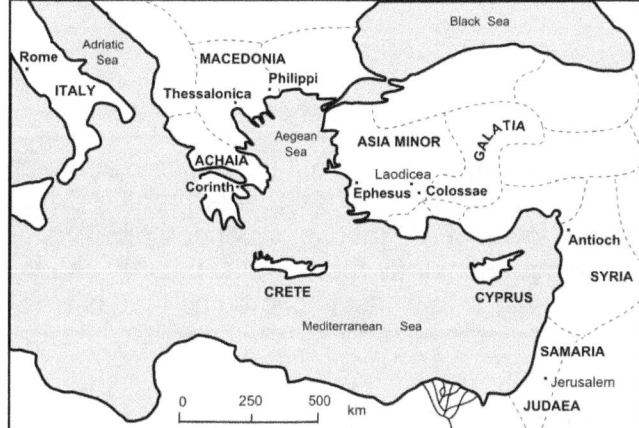

Focus on the Meaning: In making his plans, Paul claimed not to have followed his "flesh" (his sinful human nature) rather than the Holy Spirit ... Paul has argued in 2 Corinthians 1:18-20 that as God is faithful, so, too, is Paul's "word." God's faithfulness is to be seen (1) in the Son of God preached in Corinth as God's unambiguous and now-eternal "Yes," and (2) in the fact of all the promises of God having been kept in the Son of God, as proclaimed by the apostles including Paul, the minister of the God who speaks unambiguously (cf. 2 Corinthians 1:13) and who keeps his promises. (*Dr. Constable's Notes on 2 Corinthians 2017 Edition,* pages 22, 24)

14. God was completely trustworthy in fulfilling His promises to them in Christ, uniting Paul with the Corinthians. This is true of all believers.

    - What did God do to set His seal of ownership on us (v. 22)?

    - What does it mean to put down a deposit or guarantee?

    - Can humans back out of a bargain?
    - Can God back out of a bargain? See v. 20.
    - So, what does God pledge or guarantee for us? See also Ephesians 1:13-14.

    Scriptural Insight: Promise and hope – the Holy Spirit is called a "deposit" or "down payment" on our salvation, giving assurance of the completion of his work. At the moment of salvation, the Spirit places you *in Christ*. This is the basis for your: 1) acceptance before God, 2) assurance of salvation, and 3) identity. And Jesus Christ lives in you through His Spirit. Through Christ's presence *in you*, you receive: 1) life (regeneration), 2) power for living, and 3) the basis of a relationship with the living God. What a truly awesome deal!

THE GOD-DEPENDENT WOMAN

15. What else did you learn as you studied 2 Corinthians 1:15-22?

> ***Dependent Living:*** Paul made plans but held them loosely. God's grace was leading him (v. 12). The Spirit drove his concern for the Corinthians so Paul wanted to check on them. Paul said in vv. 19-20 that he depended on Christ as he made plans. Making plans then having to change them may result in disappointments and misunderstandings for those involved. Paul had to trust in Christ to overcome that as well.

What application will you make?

Respond to the Lord about what He has shown you today.

Day Four Study

Read 2 Corinthians 1:23-2:13. Ask the Lord Jesus to teach you through His Word.

What does the Bible say?

16. Paul continues to explain himself so they can understand him.

   Why had Paul not returned to Corinth first as he planned (v. 23 and 2:1)?

   Paul reminds them that his role is to do what (v. 24)?

   Why had Paul written a letter (2:3)?

LESSON TWO

As he wrote, how did he feel (2:4)?

What was true about the one who had been confronted with a deliberate sin (v. 5)?

What was true about the punishment inflicted on the offender (v. 6)?

Now what should they do (vv. 7-8)?

What might happen if they don't forgive?

For what other reason had Paul written the severe letter (v. 9)?

Paul will do what (v. 10)?

What did he hope to avoid (v. 11)?

What happened when Paul left Ephesus and went to Troas (vv. 12-13)?

Did anything else grab your attention?

What does it mean?

17. Instead of another visit (2:1), Paul wrote a painful letter. What was his concern now (vv. 2-3)?

18. Notice the number of times joy / glad / rejoice are used in 2 Corinthians 1:23-2:4. What is it about broken relationships that affects our joy?

35

Focus on the Meaning: Paul refers to "joy" repeatedly in this letter, referring to it as "overflowing" and "boundless." Only the Lord Jesus Christ can fill our hearts with overflowing joy even in the midst of hardships.

19. Correcting someone's error in behavior or thinking is hard but necessary in the church of Christ. We don't know what had happened, but we can look at an incident requiring previous correction. Read 1 Corinthians 5:1-7.

    - What was the problem that time?

    - Why is it necessary to address ungodly behavior in a church community?

    - What is the goal of caring enough about your church community that you would ask someone to leave who is deliberately sinning in such a public, proud way?

20. Based on 2 Corinthians 2:6-10, what are some "tough love" steps you can take to restore an offending community member and then comfort them?

21. Read v. 11 in several Bible translations to help in your understanding.

    Paul warned of a danger always threatening believers, especially unity within the local church community. Satan's schemes could outwit church leaders.

    - What is a scheme?

    - What does it mean to outwit?

    - What might it look like for Satan to "outwit" church leaders when it comes to enabling bad influences to remain in the church community?

LESSON TWO

> **Focus on the Meaning:** Comfort means encouragement plus alleviation of grief. The one offended must go to the offender who has been confronted and give forgiveness and comfort to her. This confirmation of love helps to bring everyone back into loving fellowship. Satan delights in seeing our church body, small groups and families broken up by our failure to forgive and confirm love.

22. Paul sent the painful letter with Titus. Read Galatians 2:1-3, Titus 1:1, 4-5, and 2 Corinthians 7:5-7. What do you learn about Titus?

> **Historical Insight:** Paul left Troas, not because he wasn't having success but because he was so concerned about his Corinthian "children." His focus was on relationship. The likely route for Titus to take back to Ephesus / Troas would have been up from Corinth to Macedonia then a short sea journey to Troas. He had places to stay along the way with the churches already planted. Paul hoped to meet Titus in Macedonia. Do you now understand why Paul started off this letter with praising God for comfort? Titus brought him comfort in the way of good news about the Corinthians.

Dependent Living: God makes you to stand firm (v. 24). You choose to let Him do so.

23. What else did you learn as you studied 2 Corinthians 1:23-2:13?

What application will you make?

24. Paul trusted Titus to represent him and help with reconciliation. Whom would you trust to send to a family member to help with reconciliation, as Paul trusted Titus? Why?

25. In what other ways can you apply this lesson to your life?

26. Review the passage for this lesson in "Day One Study." Add reasons why God wants us to depend on Him more than on ourselves to the chart below. I have given a few prompts.

Verse(s)	Reasons why God wants us to depend on Him more than on ourselves
1:17	We get distracted and disappointed when things don't go as we planned
1:22	He owns us and lives in us.
2:1-5	
2:6-10	
2:11	

Respond to the Lord about what He has shown you today.

As His child, God transforms your life by teaching you to live dependently on Him in weakness and in strength.

Recommended: Listen to "Depending on God in the Pain of Relationships" to reinforce what you have learned. Use the following listener guide.

LESSON TWO

PODCAST LISTENER GUIDE

Depending on God in the Pain of Relationships

According to 2 Corinthians 1:12-17, the opposite of dependent living is relying on worldly wisdom and making plans in a worldly manner.

AVOID WORLDLY WISDOM

> "Worldly" refers to something that proceeds from the flesh rather than the Spirit. The flesh is that part of the human nature that is controlled by sin. *Romans 8:5-8*

- The flesh is at war with God. It doesn't want to submit to God's way of approaching life. It doesn't want to please God nor can it do so. Worldly means humanistic—what humans determine to do in opposition to God and to please themselves.

- Wisdom refers to knowledge, intelligence and learning. That is neutral. You can have godly wisdom or worldly wisdom. You recognize worldly wisdom through knowing what God's way of approaching life is. You get that through studying the Bible and responding to the Holy Spirit's teaching you from the inside.

- Worldly wisdom likes to use persuasive and haughty words to gain influence and control over someone who is "less learned." Paul chose to write words that the Corinthians could read and understand. That is transparency and godly wisdom, not words to make them feel stupid. They could trust what he wrote them from a distance because they knew him.

- Like Paul, we must beware of using worldly wisdom in dealing with people or even teaching them about matters pertaining to God. Speaking truth from the Bible and using God-given logic is good. Compromising with their ideas in order to feel accepted is not.

AVOID MAKING PLANS IN A WORLDLY MANNER

- Making plans in a worldly manner means to make promises that you can't keep or won't keep. It is making promises just to pacify someone. It is lying to them. It is also being arrogant about having control of our lives.

> "Now listen, you who say, 'Today or tomorrow we will go to this or that city, spend a year there, carry on business and make money.' Why, you do not even know what will happen tomorrow. Instead, you ought to say, "'If it is the Lord's will, we will live and do this or that.'" (James 4:13-15)

- Whenever you need to make plans about things that will matter, follow this process:
    - ✓ Align yourself with the purposes of God as described in His Word.
    - ✓ Consider options that also align with the purposes of God.
    - ✓ Ask God for direction and for Him to show you the best choice.
    - ✓ Submit to God's direction and be confident in that. That is relying on Him.
    - ✓ Hold them loosely and submit to any changes that God makes along the way.

- If God does change your plans, stay focused on who you are and what God is doing in your life rather than being disappointed because things don't go your way. God always follows through with the plans that He has for every believer. He is a trustworthy God. We can submit to His direction for our plans. We can be trustworthy representatives of our trustworthy God when we are relying on Him more than on ourselves. It is a win/win.

RECONCILING RELATIONSHIPS IN A GODLY MANNER

- People will get disappointed. Broken relationships do hurt. Paul longed to be reconciled to the Corinthians. Not being with them face-to-face and only hearing about their misunderstanding of Paul's intentions caused him great distress and anguish of heart and many tears because he loved them so much. Yet, he continued to teach them truth and to demonstrate his love for them. He didn't get all huffy and give up on them.

- When our feelings are hurt, we need to learn how to reconcile relationships in a godly manner. That also requires depending on the Lord to show us how and to give us the patience to do it right. And God gives us comfort through the process.

DOES DEPENDING ON GOD MEAN THAT YOU WILL NEVER BE SAD AGAIN?

True or False? *"Depend only on God for your happiness, and you'll never be sad again."* **FALSE**

- God does not promise us the "good happenings" kind of happiness. He does promise us joy—having a deep inner gladness regardless of the circumstances going on around you. You can have a feeling of gladness or pleasure deep down inside. Biblical joy is supernatural, is inseparable from the character of God, and comes only from a relationship with Him.

- Sadness is not a bad thing. Perfectly sinless Jesus was sad at times as He grieved over death and over Jerusalem's rejection of Him. He experienced human sadness by His own choice. Sadness over sin is a good thing. It leads to repentance and reconciliation of relationship. Sadness over broken relationships leads to doing everything to reconcile the relationship.

REASONS WHY GOD WANTS US TO DEPEND ON HIM MORE THAN ON OURSELVES

- ✓ We get distracted and disappointed when things don't go as we plan. (1:17)
- ✓ He is faithful to His promises to us. (1:20)
- ✓ He owns us and lives in us. (1:22)
- ✓ To reconcile relationships rightly when our feelings are hurt. (2:1-4)
- ✓ To execute tough love when a Christian is deliberately sinning. (2:5-10)
- ✓ To keep Satan from getting an advantage over us. (2:11)

Let Jesus satisfy your heart with confidence that you can depend on Him. Then, live each day as a God-dependent woman!

3: Connect and Impart for God's Glory

2 Corinthians 2:14-4:6

You yourselves are our letter, written on our hearts, known and read by everyone. You show that you are a letter from Christ, the result of our ministry, written not with ink but with the Spirit of the living God, not on tablets of stone but on tablets of human hearts. (2 Corinthians 3:2-3)

Paul made plans to visit the Corinthians but held onto them loosely as he left them in the Lord's hands. The Spirit drove Paul's concern for the Corinthians so he changed plans to check on them. Because of God's grace leading him, he chose to delay the visit. This caused disappointments and misunderstandings for those involved. But Paul had to trust in Christ to overcome that as well.

Broken relationships due to misunderstandings and gossip from those who don't know the facts can cause great pain. Paul asks the Corinthians to assume good will, listen to wisdom, and do what is right in God's sight. Then, trust the Lord to heal the relationship as each party loves the other sincerely.

Questions to consider this week:

- If the fragrance or aroma we spread to others is the knowledge of Christ, how do we do that?
- How would you determine if someone is peddling the word of God for profit or not?
- If you are a living letter of Christ, who is reading you? Are they reading a letter that brings glory to Christ or to something else?

THE GOD-DEPENDENT WOMAN

DAY ONE STUDY—GET THE BIG PICTURE

Ask the Lord Jesus to teach you through His Word.

Read the Bible passage below (NIV). Use your own method (colored pencils, lines, shapes) to mark 1) anything that grabs your attention, 2) words you want to understand, and 3) topics you have seen before in this letter. Draw arrows between thoughts that connect. Put a star ✱ next to anything you think relates to dependent living.

2 12 Now when I went to Troas to preach the gospel of Christ and found that the Lord had opened a door for me, 13 I still had no peace of mind, because I did not find my brother Titus there. So I said goodbye to them and went on to Macedonia.

14 But thanks be to God, who always leads us in Christ's triumphal procession and uses us to spread the aroma of the knowledge of him everywhere. 15 For we are to God the pleasing aroma of Christ among those who are being saved and those who are perishing. 16 To the one we are an aroma that brings death; to the other, an aroma that brings life. And who is equal to such a task? 17 Unlike so many, we do not peddle the word of God for profit. On the contrary, in Christ we speak before God with sincerity, as those sent from God.

3 Are we beginning to commend ourselves again? Or do we need, like some people, letters of recommendation to you or from you? 2 You yourselves are our letter, written on our hearts, known and read by everyone. 3 You show that you are a letter from Christ, the result of our ministry, written not with ink but with the Spirit of the living God, not on tablets of stone but on tablets of human hearts.

4 Such confidence we have through Christ before God. 5 Not that we are competent in ourselves to claim anything for ourselves, but our competence comes from God. 6 He has made us competent as ministers of a new covenant—not of the letter but of the Spirit; for the letter kills, but the Spirit gives life.

7 Now if the ministry that brought death, which was engraved in letters on stone, came with glory, so that the Israelites could not look steadily at the face of Moses because of its glory, transitory though it was, 8 will not the ministry of the Spirit be even more glorious? 9 If the ministry that brought condemnation was glorious, how much more glorious is the ministry that brings righteousness! 10 For what was glorious has no glory now in comparison with the surpassing glory. 11 And if what was transitory came with glory, how much greater is the glory of that which lasts!

12 Therefore, since we have such a hope, we are very bold. 13 We are not like Moses, who would put a veil over his face to prevent the Israelites from seeing the end of what was passing away. 14 But their minds were made dull, for to this day the same veil remains when the old covenant is read. It has not been removed, because only in Christ is it taken away. 15 Even to this day when Moses is read, a veil covers their hearts. 16 But whenever anyone turns to the Lord, the veil is taken away. 17 Now the Lord is the Spirit, and where the Spirit of the Lord is, there is freedom. 18 And we all, who with unveiled faces contemplate the Lord's glory, are being transformed into his image with ever-increasing glory, which comes from the Lord, who is the Spirit.

4 Therefore, since through God's mercy we have this ministry, we do not lose heart. 2 Rather, we have renounced secret and shameful ways; we do not use deception, nor do we distort the word of God. On the contrary, by setting forth the truth plainly we commend ourselves to everyone's conscience in the sight of God. 3 And even if our gospel is veiled, it is veiled to those who are perishing. 4 The god of this age has blinded the minds of unbelievers, so that they cannot see the light of the gospel that displays the glory of Christ, who is the image of God. 5 For what

LESSON THREE

we preach is not ourselves, but Jesus Christ as Lord, and ourselves as your servants for Jesus' sake. 6 For God, who said, "Let light shine out of darkness," made his light shine in our hearts to give us the light of the knowledge of God's glory displayed in the face of Christ.

1. What grabbed your attention from these verses?
   - 2:14-17

   - 3:1-6

   - 3:7-4:6

2. What verses or specific words do you want to understand better?

3. What topics are repeated in this passage or continue an earlier discussion in this letter?

4. What verses illustrate or help you understand what dependent living on God looks like?

Respond to the Lord about what He has shown you today.

THE GOD-DEPENDENT WOMAN

DAY TWO STUDY

Read 2 Corinthians 2:14-17. Ask the Lord Jesus to teach you through His Word.

> **Historical Insight:** Paul was an observer of his world and often included references to the culture as illustrations for his listeners. The imagery is that of a Roman triumph (victory parade) in which the victorious general would lead his soldiers and the captives they had taken in festive procession, while the people watched and applauded and the air was filled with the sweet smell released by burning of spices in the street. (*NIV Study Bible,* note on v. 14, p. 1765)

What does the Bible say?

5. Corinth was a Roman colony. Roman parades were special to them. Consider the "Historical Insight" information above as you answer the following questions.

    Who is the victorious general leading us (v. 14)?

    Who are the ones following Him (v. 14)?

    ✱ What does God do through us (v. 14)?

    We are what to God (v. 15)?

    To whom are we the aroma / fragrance that brings life (vv. 15-16)?

    To whom are we the aroma / fragrance of death (vv. 15-16)?

    As one who spreads the aroma of the knowledge of God, what does Paul not do (v. 17)?

    Instead, what does Paul do?

    Did anything else grab your attention?

    > **Think About It:** The sobering fact is that the fragrance of Christ is glorious to those who desire Him as Savior, but to those who reject Him, the scent is loathsome. (Kelly Minter, *All Things New,* page. 44)

LESSON THREE

What does it mean?

6. Paul says that the fragrance we spread is the knowledge of Christ, the aroma of Christ.

    - Describe an aroma that is especially enticing or inviting to you.

    - How can we be such an aroma to others? See Colossians 4:5-6 and other verses you know that illustrate this.

    Scriptural Insight: Paul asks the rhetorical question, "Who is equal to such a task (v. 16)?" He knows that no one is. Our responsibility to represent Christ well and be that enticing aroma is weighty. But God does not ask us to do what He does not enable us to do. God makes us competent to share Him with others. See 2 Corinthians 3:5.

7. Read Acts 18:1-7, 1 Corinthians 9:11-15; and 2 Corinthians 11:7-9. Traveling teachers in that culture usually expected to be paid for their services.

    From the Greek: The underlying Greek word *kapelos* (translated peddling / marketing) referred to a huckster—one who sells or advertises something in an aggressive, dishonest, or annoying way. Such hucksters often corrupted their goods with impurities to make more money.

    ✱ What was Paul's practice with the Corinthians instead of "peddling the word of God for profit?"

    ✱ From 2 Corinthians 2:14-17, what is the motive and drive of Paul and his team if not for money (profit)?

    Scriptural Insight: How is Paul able confidently to attribute such negative motives to these men, while expecting his own claim "of sincerity" to be accepted? It appears that he is appealing to the known fact that these men have received some material benefit from the Corinthians (2 Corinthians 11:20), whereas Paul deliberately refused payment from them (2 Corinthians 11:7-12; 12:13-16). (*Dr. Constable's Notes on 2 Corinthians 2017 Edition,* p. 35)

8. What else did you learn as you studied 2 Corinthians 2:14-17?

THE GOD-DEPENDENT WOMAN

What application will you make?

God uses our words and actions to bring out what people are already thinking about Him. Their responses to us are often an indicator of where they are spiritually—and that can be good or bad, positive or negative. If they are seeking to know more about Christ, they may be drawn to His fragrance in us. If someone is mad at God, we may experience that anger directed at us.

9. How do you respond when someone attacks your faith? How does it help to consider they may be reacting more to God than to you?

10. How would you recognize someone peddling the word of God for profit? What questions would you ask to determine if someone is peddling the word of God for profit or sincerely serving the Lord Jesus in ministry?

11. In what other ways can you apply this lesson to your life?

Dependent Living: Our God leads us and uses us to draw others to Christ and His victory parade. We let Him lead us and use us according to His will.

Respond to the Lord about what He has shown you today.

LESSON THREE

DAY THREE STUDY

Read 2 Corinthians 3:1-6. Ask the Lord Jesus to teach you through His Word.

What does the Bible say?

> **Historical Insight:** In Acts 18:27 and Romans 16:1, we see examples of letters of recommendation. The appearance of vagrant impostors, who claimed to be teachers of apostolic truth, led to the need for letters of recommendation. Paul needed no such confirmation; but others, including the Corinthian intruders, did need authentication and, being themselves, false, often resorted to unscrupulous methods for obtaining or forging letters of recommendation. (*NIV Study Bible,* note on 3:1, p. 1765)

12. Have you needed a letter of recommendation for something? Paul's credentials have been questioned. Some were saying that he needs a letter of recommendation (v. 1).

    The Corinthians are what for Paul (v. 2)?

    They show what (v. 3)? Note: This is a "Trinity" verse supporting the doctrine of one God in three persons (God who is the Father, Christ, and the Spirit).

    ✱ Paul gets this confidence how (v. 4)?

    ✱ Paul says, "Our competence is not (v. 5) _____,

    but our competence comes _____."

    ✱ God has made Paul and his companions competent as what (v. 6)?

    Did anything else grab your attention?

> **Focus on the Meaning:** About 3:6—The Old Covenant killed people in the sense that it showed how impossible it was to measure up to God's requirements. Moreover, it announced a death sentence on all who fell short of complete obedience (cf. Rom. 7:9-11; Gal. 3:10). (Dr. *Constable's Notes on 2 Corinthians 2023 edition,* page 56)

What does it mean?

13. Read vv. 2-3 in several Bible translations. Summarize what Paul is saying.

THE GOD-DEPENDENT WOMAN

14. Read 1 Corinthians 9:1-2 and Acts 9:15-16; 18:9-10 for background to what Paul says here. What are Paul's credentials?

15. ✱ How do his credentials give him both confidence (trust, reliance) and competence / sufficiency in the work that Jesus gave him to do (2 Corinthians 1:1; 2:17; 3:5-6)?

> **From the Greek:** The Greek word *hikonas* ("to have enough") is translated in vv. 5-6 as competent (NIV), adequate (NAS), qualified (NLT), and sufficient (ESV/KJV). God is the one who makes anyone "have enough" for the work He has called her to do.

16. What else did you learn as you studied 2 Corinthians 3:1-6?

What application will you make?

17. In the gospels, we see that Jesus would connect with people and impart truth to them. You are His letter for others to read. And He has used His servants to reach you and model for you how to follow Him.

- Who has modeled for you how to follow Christ? Who has written on your life?

- What do you hope people read in your letter? Is there anything in your letter that says you rely more on yourself than on Christ?

- Who are your letters, those in whom you are consciously investing right now?

18. God is the one who makes you competent / sufficient / adequate for the work that Jesus gives you to do. Is there something right now That is in front of you—a need, a challenge, an opportunity—but you feel spiritually incompetent to do it? How do these verses today speak to your situation?

19. In what other ways can you apply this lesson to your life?

Respond to the Lord about what He has shown you today.

Day Four Study

Read 2 Corinthians 3:7-4:6. Ask the Lord Jesus to teach you through His Word.

What does the Bible say?

20. Paul contrasts the Old Covenant with the New Covenant, revealing how life with the Spirit of God is so much better.

    Count the number of times "glory," "glorious," "radiance," "light" and "shine" are used. _____

    Count the number of times "veil" or "covering" is used. _____

    What is the condition of the Jews who have not trusted in Christ (3:14-15)?

    Where the Spirit of the Lord Jesus is, there is freedom from what (3:14,16)?

    ✱ As we contemplate or behold the Lord's glory, what is the Spirit doing to us (3:18)?

THE GOD-DEPENDENT WOMAN

Knowing God gave Paul his ministry through His mercy, how does he respond (4:1)?

What has Paul renounced and chosen not to do (4:2)?

✱ On the contrary, what does he do (4:2)?

The god of this age (Satan) does what (4:4)?

Paul doesn't preach himself but preaches what (4:5)?

For God did what (4:6)?

Did anything else grab your attention?

> **Focus on the Meaning:** Freedom is being out in the open; it is the boldness of having nothing to hide. The woman who is free has no reputation to defend, no image to hide behind, nothing to preserve about herself. She can be herself. (Ray Stedman, adapted from *Authentic Christianity*)

What does it mean?

21. Contrast the Old Covenant (the Law) with the New Covenant of the Spirit (3:7-11).

The Old Covenant	The New Covenant

> **Focus on the Meaning:** You may be a Christian, appreciating God's grace for salvation and heaven, but thinking that you need to be "under the law" in your Christian life. Why would you sense that? Perhaps you feel your relationship with God is based upon your performance, that His love for you is conditional, or that you're never "good enough" for Him to really accept you. That's Old Covenant thinking. Read this passage again and realize that God wants to set you free from that inner turmoil. The New Covenant is His gift to you. (Steve Hixon)

LESSON THREE

22. Paul says in v. 18 that we are being *"transformed"* by the Spirit. The original Greek word means "to change from one form to another." For us, we are being transformed into the image of Christ … not in our faces but in our characters.

- What were we like before trusting in Christ? Read 2 Corinthians 4:4 and Ephesians 2:1-3.

- How are we transformed into the image of Christ by the Spirit? Read Romans 12:2 and Colossians 3:12-17. Recognize that how the Spirit works is part mystery. We can know with confidence that He works in us. We are to respond to His Word and leading as He does.

Scriptural Insight: The "image" of God, that we see in the Word, accurately reflects God, though we do not yet see God Himself. What we see in the "mirror" of God's Word is the Lord [Jesus], not ourselves. We experience gradual transformation … not in our faces but in our characters (cf. 2 Peter 3:18). (*Dr. Constable's Notes on 2 Corinthians 2017 Edition*, p. 43)

The concept of glory can be hard to understand. But Paul uses it repeatedly in this passage so let us at least try.

From the Greek: "Glory" comes from the Greek word, *doxa*, meaning "good opinion resulting in praise and honor; splendor, brightness, majesty."

23. Why will being transformed into the Lord's image bring "ever-increasing glory" to us rather than fading glory? See 2 Corinthians 1:21; 3:18; and 4:6.

Scriptural Insight: We are made holy in God's sight at the moment of salvation. Holy ones are called saints (2 Corinthians 1:1). During our life on earth, we are also "being made holy" in our thoughts, words, and actions by the work of the Holy Spirit (2 Corinthians 3:18). This is ongoing from the moment of salvation until the Lord comes or the believer dies, when our "being made holy" is complete (Philippians 1:6). The goal of the Spirit's work is to transform us into the likeness of Christ (2 Corinthians 3:18) so that we become in thought and behavior what we are in status—holy as God is holy.

THE GOD-DEPENDENT WOMAN

24. Although Moses wore a physical "veil" to cover the fading glory from his face, Paul uses "veil" in a figurative sense to represent the stubborn refusal of the Jews to believe the gospel message. He says that Satan ("the god of this age") veils the gospel by blinding the minds of unbelievers (as in 2 Corinthians 3:14-16 for the Jews).

- The underlying Greek word means "to blunt the mental discernment, to darken the mind." Why does Satan do that?

- How do you think he does that? In other words, what would it look like to blind someone's mind?

- Who removes the veil / blindness? How? Give verses from this passage. See also Acts 26:17-18 and Colossians 1:12-13.

Scriptural Insight: In the Bible, there always seems to be a period of darkness before there comes a light. According to the Hebrew calendar—the one Jesus used—a day starts at sunset and not at midnight or sunrise. So even the Hebrew day begins with night. Isn't that interesting? During dark times, dawn will always come. All around us it is easy to see the darkness present in this world. Wickedness, greed, selfishness, cold-blooded violence... the darkness can quickly overwhelm a soul. But there is hope! Isaiah 9:2 predicted that those living in darkness would see a great light. Jesus was that light. And when you look at His life in the Gospel books you can see that He broke the darkness that was present in His land. He healed sick people, taught the curious how to live a life of purpose, and forgave the sins of those who were longing to be free from their guilt. He still does the same today. Our world is not completely dark. There is light that always dawns. (John Newton, *Advent for Restless Hearts,* p. 12)

25. What else did you learn as you studied 2 Corinthians 3:7-4:6?

LESSON THREE

What application will you make?

26. As living letters of Christ, we reflect the glory of Christ. What has the Spirit changed in you since you trusted in Christ so that you reflect His glory more than your own?

27. When given the opportunity, are you prepared to share the gospel message to someone who has been living in blindness? Write out the basic gospel message in the space below. [In the "Resources" section at the end of this study guide, you can see several ways to word it.] Get to know it well and ask the Lord Jesus to give you an opportunity to share this good news with someone who needs to hear it.

28. In what other ways can you apply this lesson to your life?

29. Review the passage for this lesson in "Day One Study." Add reasons why God wants us to depend on Him more than on ourselves to the chart below. I have given a few prompts.

Verse(s)	Reasons why God wants us to depend on Him more than on ourselves
2:14	*He uses us to spread the knowledge of Him.*
2:17	*He sends us to speak for Him.*
3:3	*He writes a letter of recommendation for Himself in our lives.*
3:4	*He gives us confidence to trust Him.*

THE GOD-DEPENDENT WOMAN

Respond to the Lord about what He has shown you today.

As His child, God transforms your life by teaching you to live dependently on Him in weakness and in strength.

> **Recommended:** Listen to "Being Transformed into the Likeness of Christ" to reinforce what you have learned. Use the following listener guide.

LESSON THREE

PODCAST LISTENER GUIDE

Being Transformed into the Likeness of Christ

GOD WANTS US TO BE AN AROMA OF LIFE

Aromas are powerful things. We ought to have an enticing smell and not a disgusting aroma. But we humans are frail. We are swayed by whatever is modeled before us and by our own emotions of how we want to act. Yet, God chooses us to be an aroma of life to others. He doesn't ask us to do what He doesn't enable us to do. God builds into our lives that which fills our hearts with Him. This makes us competent to represent Him to others.

GOD FILLS OUR HEARTS WITH HIMSELF AND MAKES US COMPETENT

You and I can have confidence because of our faith in Jesus Christ. From the moment of our salvation, God Himself comes to live inside of us in the form of the Holy Spirit.

Who the Holy Spirit is

The Holy Spirit is the third person of the Trinity. Our God is one God but three persons. The Spirit is not an impersonal "it" or simply an influence but a personal being just as the Father and the Son are persons. He convicts the unbeliever of sin and makes believers into new creations the moment we believe. He is the first gift we receive from God when we trust in Jesus for salvation.

What He does for us

[For a more complete explanation, listen to the podcast for *Radical Acts Bible Study,* Lesson 2.]

- Spirit Baptism is the Spirit's work of indwelling the believer. Every believer receives the complete Holy Spirit the moment we trust in Christ. He enters our spirits and seals us with Himself so our salvation is secure. He is God's empowering presence in us. He enables us to understand the Bible and takes our prayer needs to God the Father, even when we can't.

- Spirit Baptism is the Spirit's work of uniting us with Christ, fusing us together with who He is and what He has done. We take on the identity of Jesus so that when God looks on us, He sees Jesus instead. All the spiritual blessings we have in Christ—being chosen, adopted, forgiven, sealed—are wrapped up and delivered to us at Spirit Baptism. It is God's gift initiated by God to those who put their faith in Christ. It is not initiated by us.

- Spirit Baptism is the Spirit's work of making all believers permanent members of the Body of Christ. *1 Corinthians 12:13*

- Spirit Baptism is a permanent condition, occurring once and for all at salvation. *Galatians 3:26-27; Ephesians 4:4-5*

- Spirit Baptism is a change of state in which we are made into new creations.

- Spirit Baptism begins the transformation process that changes you into the likeness of Christ from the inside out so that your character looks more like Jesus and your lifestyle brings God's glory to everyone who is watching. *2 Corinthians 3:17-18*

Transformation into the Likeness of Christ Brings God's Glory to Others

There are two aspects of being transformed to the likeness of Christ. God's part and our part.

- God's part involves mystery about how He does it. The Scriptures teach that He works according to His will and purpose for your life.

- Our part involves choices. 1) One choice is renewing your mind (Romans 12:2) through studying God's Words in the Bible to see how to approach life His way. The Holy Spirit uses the Word to transform you. 2) Another choice on your part is having a desire for God's work in you to give you the character of Christ. When you long for His work in your life, you will want to submit to what He is doing and ask for Him to change you. 3) A third choice is to commit to doing life God's way. That is part of the transformation process. Jesus modeled for us how to approach life God's way and live in dependence upon Him in the process. Living in dependence means you choose to trust Him in prayer.

- God will complete His part—both during your lifetime as you yield to His work in your life and after your life on earth ends as you begin your life in heaven. You become God's letter of recommendation from Himself to the world. Others seeing the transformation in you now brings God's glory to them. And His glory can be evident even if you have problems in your own lives because it is not about you. It is about Christ in you.

Jesus Christ gave His life for you so He can give His life to you so He can live His life through you. (Major Ian Thomas, *Saving Life of Christ*)

Does it all depend on me while I am depending on God?

True or False? *"It all depends on me, and I depend on God."*   **FALSE**

Control is an illusion. You can only control what you choose to do in response to any situation. You have no control over circumstances, what happens in the world, the choices others make, and even your own schedule. Jesus Christ is the Lord of planet Earth. All "its" are under His domain, not yours. Now, don't you feel better?

Reasons why God wants us to depend on Him more than on ourselves

- ✓ He uses us to spread the knowledge of Him. (2:14)
- ✓ He sends us to speak for Him. (2:17)
- ✓ He writes a letter of recommendation for Himself in our lives. (3:3)
- ✓ He gives us confidence to trust Him. (3:4)
- ✓ He gives us competence to represent Him. (3:5)
- ✓ He takes away the veil over our hearts when we believe. (3:16)
- ✓ He transforms us by His Spirit. (3:18)
- ✓ So we won't lose heart. (4:1)
- ✓ He makes His light shine in the darkness through us. (4:6)

Let Jesus satisfy your heart with confidence that you can depend on Him. Then, live each day as a God-dependent woman!

LESSON FOUR

4: Let God's Light Shine

2 Corinthians 4:7-5:10

But we have this treasure in jars of clay to show that this all-surpassing power is from God and not from us. (2 Corinthians 4:7, Memory Verse #2)

In Lesson 3, you learned that you are the aroma of God spreading everywhere the knowledge of Him. Women know all about aroma. Think of the delightful smell of good food cooking or fine perfume, and of course, the many benefits of essential oils. A pleasing aroma influences and invites the receiver to enjoy more of the same. So it is with you as the aroma of Christ.

You are also a living letter presenting Christ to those who are "reading" you. Have you thought about how much reading stimulates the mind and draws one into exploring more? That is what the Spirit of God is writing in your life, a letter that others will want to read and experience what you have in Christ.

You are an illustration of the freedom that comes in Christ—freedom from the blindness enslaving the mind of an unbelieving person. As you are transformed by the Holy Spirit into the image of Christ, you are freed from sinful behaviors so that your life will glorify God more and more. To glorify God means to enhance His reputation. That is what we are to do with our lives.

But whether you will be a delightful aroma, an inviting letter, or a clear image of Christ depends on how much you are relying on God to lead you and change you.

Yet, your aroma of God and letter of Christ are emanating from frail human bodies. The best news is that God overcomes your weaknesses with His power as you trust in Him.

Questions to consider this week:

- How do you keep your eyes fixed on what is unseen and eternal rather than seen and temporary (4:18)?

- Why does God put His treasure in "jars of clay?" And what is revealed in our frail human bodies during every trial that threatens us?

- What will it take for you to trust in God to help you view whatever hardships and pain you experience as "light and momentary troubles?"

THE GOD-DEPENDENT WOMAN

DAY ONE STUDY—GET THE BIG PICTURE

Ask the Lord Jesus to teach you through His Word.

Read the Bible passage below (NIV, including verses from the last lesson). Use your own method (colored pencils, lines, shapes) to mark 1) anything that grabs your attention, 2) words you want to understand, and 3) topics you have seen before in this letter. Draw arrows between thoughts that connect. Put a star ✱ next to anything you think relates to dependent living.

3 18 And we all, who with unveiled faces contemplate the Lord's glory, are being transformed into his image with ever-increasing glory, which comes from the Lord, who is the Spirit.

4 Therefore, since through God's mercy we have this ministry, we do not lose heart. 2 Rather, we have renounced secret and shameful ways; we do not use deception, nor do we distort the word of God. On the contrary, by setting forth the truth plainly we commend ourselves to everyone's conscience in the sight of God. 3 And even if our gospel is veiled, it is veiled to those who are perishing. 4 The god of this age has blinded the minds of unbelievers, so that they cannot see the light of the gospel that displays the glory of Christ, who is the image of God. 5 For what we preach is not ourselves, but Jesus Christ as Lord, and ourselves as your servants for Jesus' sake. 6 For God, who said, "Let light shine out of darkness," made his light shine in our hearts to give us the light of the knowledge of God's glory displayed in the face of Christ.

7 But we have this treasure in jars of clay to show that this all-surpassing power is from God and not from us. 8 We are hard pressed on every side, but not crushed; perplexed, but not in despair; 9 persecuted, but not abandoned; struck down, but not destroyed. 10 We always carry around in our body the death of Jesus, so that the life of Jesus may also be revealed in our body. 11 For we who are alive are always being given over to death for Jesus' sake, so that his life may also be revealed in our mortal body. 12 So then, death is at work in us, but life is at work in you.

13 It is written: "I believed; therefore I have spoken." Since we have that same spirit of faith, we also believe and therefore speak, 14 because we know that the one who raised the Lord Jesus from the dead will also raise us with Jesus and present us with you to himself. 15 All this is for your benefit, so that the grace that is reaching more and more people may cause thanksgiving to overflow to the glory of God.

16 Therefore we do not lose heart. Though outwardly we are wasting away, yet inwardly we are being renewed day by day. 17 For our light and momentary troubles are achieving for us an eternal glory that far outweighs them all. 18 So we fix our eyes not on what is seen, but on what is unseen, since what is seen is temporary, but what is unseen is eternal.

5 For we know that if the earthly tent we live in is destroyed, we have a building from God, an eternal house in heaven, not built by human hands. 2 Meanwhile we groan, longing to be clothed instead with our heavenly dwelling, 3 because when we are clothed, we will not be found naked. 4 For while we are in this tent, we groan and are burdened, because we do not wish to be unclothed but to be clothed instead with our heavenly dwelling, so that what is mortal may be swallowed up by life. 5 Now the one who has fashioned us for this very purpose is God, who has given us the Spirit as a deposit, guaranteeing what is to come.

6 Therefore we are always confident and know that as long as we are at home in the body we are away from the Lord. 7 For we live by faith, not by sight. 8 We are confident, I say, and would prefer to be away from the body and at home with the Lord. 9 So we make it our goal to please him, whether we are at home in the body or away from it. 10 For we must all appear before the judgment seat of Christ, so that each of us may receive what is due us for the things done while in the body, whether good or bad.

LESSON FOUR

1. What grabbed your attention from these verses?
   - 4:7-12

   - 4:13-18

   - 5:1-10

2. What verses or specific words do you want to understand better?

3. What topics are repeated in this passage or continue an earlier discussion in this letter?

4. What verses illustrate or help you understand what dependent living on God looks like?

Respond to the Lord about what He has shown you today.

THE GOD-DEPENDENT WOMAN

Day Two Study

Read 2 Corinthians 4:7-12. Ask the Lord Jesus to teach you through His Word.

What does the Bible say?

5. Answer the following questions based on what is written in the biblical text.

   Why does God put His treasure in "jars of clay" (4:7)?

   From 4:8-9, fill out this chart.

We are …	but not …
We are …	but not …
We are …	but not …
We are …	but not …

   What is revealed in our frail human bodies during every trial that threatens us (vv. 10-11)?

   Did anything else grab your attention?

What does it mean?

> **Historical Insight:** The pottery lamps which could be bought for a coin or two in the Corinthian market-place provided a sufficient analogy; it did not matter how cheap or fragile they were so long as they showed the light. (*Dr. Constable's Notes on 2 Corinthians 2017 Edition*, p. 49)

6. Let's try to understand what Paul means by "the treasure" in 4:7. From 3:18-4:6, what could be "the treasure" in 4:7? Also look at other Bible translations of 4:7 for help in understanding this verse.

> **Think About It:** The light-bearer is weak, BUT the light is strong!

LESSON FOUR

7. ✱ How does 2 Corinthians 4:7 relate to 4:8-9? See also 3:18.

   Think About It: There will be times when you feel like you're going crazy, struggling, and wondering how you'll ever *live* through your hardships or heartaches. Take it from a veteran: do *not* let yourself sink into despair. Set the bar high in your battle against despondency by holding onto biblical hope. Find an anchor in Scripture, such as a favorite psalm or snippet of a proverb. Pick a timeless stanza from a hymn or chorus. Use that Scripture or song as your stake in the ground, your resolute act of defiance against discouragement. And, above all, trust in God. (Joni Eareckson Tada, *Just Between Us,* Fall 2018, p. 8)

8. To understand vv. 10-11 better, see Galatians 2:20 and 2 Corinthians 5:7. This is the life of faith and dependent living. Who gives His life to us? _____ Whose life is being lived through us? _____ From where do we get the ability to live this way?

   Focus on the Meaning: Jesus Christ gave His life *for* you, so He could give His life *to* you, so He could live His life *through* you. (Major Ian Thomas, T*he Saving Life of Christ*)

9. So, why does God put His treasure in jars of clay? See also 4:15.

10. What else did you learn as you studied 2 Corinthians 4:7-12?

What application will you make?

11. Read the "Think About It" below. Is this how you think of yourself? Why or why not?

    Think About It: A vessel's worth comes from what it holds, not from what it is. Paul contrasted the relative insignificance and unattractiveness of the light-bearers with the surpassing worth and beauty of the light (i.e., God's glory). ... It is precisely the Christian's utter frailty which lays him open to the experience of the all-sufficiency of God's grace, so that he is able even to rejoice because of his weakness (2 Corinthians 12:9)—something that astonishes and baffles the world, which thinks only in terms of human ability. (*Dr. Constable's Notes on 2 Corinthians 2017 Edition,* pages 49-50)

THE GOD-DEPENDENT WOMAN

12. In what other ways can you apply this lesson to your life?

Respond to the Lord about what He has shown you today.

DAY THREE STUDY

Read 2 Corinthians 4:13-18. Ask the Lord Jesus to teach you through His Word.

What does the Bible say?

13. Answer the following questions based on what is written in the biblical text.

Why do Paul and his team continue to speak in spite of the dangers (vv. 13-14)?

How do the Corinthians benefit from Paul continuing to preach Christ (v. 15)?

Why do they not lose heart (see also 4:1) even during their struggles (v. 16)?

What does Paul call the painful times he's experienced (v. 17)?

What are those troubles achieving for him?

What does he do to keep going (v. 18)?

Did anything else grab your attention?

LESSON FOUR

What does this mean?

14. Paul quotes Psalm 116 in v.13. Read Psalm 116:5-10. What has the psalmist learned about life that relates to Paul's experience?

Think About It: The resurrection of Christ is the greatest event in human history. No one was resurrected with an immortal body before that time or has been since. The great hope for us is that we will be resurrected when Jesus comes. We will be presented to God with all believers and live in God's presence for the rest of eternity (v. 14).

15. Paul mentions "not losing heart" twice in this chapter (vv. 1, 16). Sometimes looking at the opposite helps us to understand.

- What does it mean to "lose heart?"

- So, what does it mean to "not lose heart?" And why is this important?

16. "Overflow" (or, flow over) is another key term in 2 Corinthians. Paul uses it 7 times. It refers to things that overflow, excel, or abound.

- Read 1:5. What overflows?

- Read 3:9. What overflows or abounds?

- Read 4:15. What overflows? Why?

17. What else did you learn as you studied 2 Corinthians 4:13-18?

THE GOD-DEPENDENT WOMAN

What application will you make?

"Light and momentary troubles." That is what Paul called his hardships and pain because he was looking beyond today and seeing the joy of being in heaven forever afterwards. After reading just part of what he experienced (we'll see lots more in chapters 6 and 11), it seems insane for him to say this. Commonly, our frail human nature would rather complain and even compare our troubles with each other to see if we have it better or worse. Have you noticed this?

18. What will it take for you to trust in God to help you view whatever hardships and pain you experience as "light and momentary troubles?" Ask Him for that right now.

19. In what other ways can you apply this lesson to your life?

Respond to the Lord about what He has shown you today.

DAY FOUR STUDY

Read 2 Corinthians 5:1-10. Ask the Lord Jesus to teach you through His Word.

What does the Bible say?

> **Historical Insight:** In ancient times, a "tent" was a familiar symbol of what was transitory. Our physical bodies are only temporary structures, but God is preparing new bodies for us, that are far superior to anything that human hands can produce and maintain. (*Dr. Constable's Notes on 2 Corinthians 2017 Edition*, p. 54)

Paul continues to give reasons why we should not lose heart by keeping our eyes fixed on what is unseen and eternal rather than seen and temporary (4:18).

LESSON FOUR

20. From the biblical text, answer the questions below.

   If our earthly tent is destroyed, we know we have what (v. 1)?

   How do we feel now (vv. 2 and 4)?

   What do we know to be true (v. 3)?

   So, what do we want to happen (v. 4)?

   What has God done (v. 5)?

   What does Paul know with confidence (vv. 6-7)?

   What would he prefer (v. 8)?

   While we live, we make it our goal to do what (v. 9)?

   For we must all appear where (v. 10?

   What do we receive there?

   Did anything else grab your attention?

What does it mean?

21. We are living in the now and the "not yet." Describe the future promise we have and the ever-present tension in a Christian's life (vv. 1-8).
    - Future promises we have …

65

- Present tension we experience …

22. Focus on 2 Corinthians 5:4. Paul wrote about this in his previous letter to the Corinthians. Read 1 Corinthians 15:53-54. What did he say?

> **Scriptural Insight:** All Christians who die will receive an immortal body (v. 1). This is by itself a substantial gift of glory. Second, all Christians, including those who die soon after becoming believers, presently possess the Holy Spirit—who is God's pledge of our future complete glorification (vv. 4-5). Third, death begins a new phase of existence for all believers, that will be far superior to what we experience now (vv. 7-8). (*Dr. Constable's Notes on 2 Corinthians 2017 Edition*, p. 54)

23. Let's look at how we are to live now in these earthly bodies (vv. 6-9). What do these statements mean?

    - Living by faith, not by sight (v. 7)

    - Living to please the Lord (v. 9 and Romans 14:7-8)

> **Think About It:** Living by faith in the Lord Jesus Christ and all He has promised for our present and our future is NOT the same thing as taking a leap in the dark. See Hebrews 11:1, 6. We can know Him through all that is revealed for us to know.

24. When our earthly bodies die, we appear before the judgment seat of Christ (v. 10). Read about this in 1 Corinthians 3:11-15. Paul is addressing believers about rewards, not salvation.

    - As already saved people, guaranteed to receive heavenly dwellings when we die, are we responsible for our actions while in our "earthly tents?" ___ Yes or ___ No

    - Why does God care about this? Use what you have already seen in 2 Corinthians.

25. What else did you learn as you studied 2 Corinthians 5:1-10?

What application will you make?

26. ✱ What confidence can you have at your death?

Do you have this confidence? _____ Trusting Christ for what happens to you after you die is another aspect of dependent living.

Scriptural Insight: Look at the chart below to gain confidence about what happens when you die.

What doesn't happen at death	***What does happen at death***
• Not annihilation (Luke 16:19-31) • Not soul sleep (Philippians 1:23) • Not floating spirit (2 Cor. 5:3) • Not reincarnation (Hebrews 9:27) • Not purgatory (Colossians 1:22)	• Fall asleep on earth; wake up in heaven (1 Thessalonians 4:14) • Leave earthly tent; get heavenly dwelling fashioned for us (2 Cor. 5:1) • Be immediately at home with the Lord (2 Cor. 5:8)

27. In what other ways can you apply this lesson to your life?

Dependent Living: Living by faith is offering yourself to God (Romans 6:13), choosing to approach life His way (seen in the New Testament writings), and trusting Him with the results.

THE GOD-DEPENDENT WOMAN

28. Review the passage for this lesson in "Day One Study." Add reasons why God wants us to depend on Him more than on ourselves to the chart below. I have given a few prompts.

Verse(s)	Reasons why God wants us to depend on Him more than on ourselves
4:7	*He can demonstrate His power through our frailty (jars of clay).*
4:8-9	*He keeps us from being crushed when we are burdened.*
4:10	*He reveals Jesus' life in and through us.*
4:16)	*He can keep us from losing heart.*

29. Did you notice that every daily lesson in this study begins and ends with prayer? God speaks to you through His word. You may respond to Him about anything and ask Him to make His word true in your life. Lack of prayer is often a sign of self-sufficiency rather than dependent living and will lead you to doing what is not pleasing in God's sight. **Spend some time responding to the Lord about what He has shown you in this whole lesson.**

As His child, God transforms your life by teaching you to live dependently on Him in weakness and in strength.

> **Recommended:** Listen to "The Purpose and Reward for Enduring Challenges of Life" to reinforce what you have learned. Use the following listener guide.

LESSON FOUR

PODCAST LISTENER GUIDE

The Purpose and Reward for Enduring Challenges of Life

GOD OVERCOMES YOUR WEAKNESSES.

- When something goes wrong, you may feel helpless as a victim of circumstances. Or you might be the person who dwells on your mistakes. You may focus on your inadequacy, not being enough of…whatever. Sadly, other people like to point out all those weaknesses in your life, too, making you feel even worse about them. Have you experienced that?

- God helps us in our weakness and works for our good according to His purpose for us. That tells me that our God has bigger purposes for our weaknesses than what we see or know each step of the way. When it comes to our circumstances, our mistakes, and our feelings of inadequacy, He asks us to trust that He is bigger than all of those.

You can know that God is bigger than your circumstances.

- Circumstances are conditions affecting our lives that are beyond our control or ability to "fix."

- Our God is faithful to not let us be crushed or destroyed even in the worst of circumstances. He doesn't abandon us. When you depend upon God to get you through them, you will likely see and appreciate God's gifts to you in a greater way.

You can know that God is bigger than your mistakes.

- Mistakes are generally two kinds. 1) Willfully going against clear Biblical guidance about what is right and wrong. 2) Attempting to "fix a problem" without clear Biblical guidance that doesn't turn out as expected.

- God has given us a mind to use for making decisions in all areas of life. So, we should pray, ask for guidance from the Holy Spirit, get advice from other believers, check to see if it's legal, then make the decision and act on it, trusting God with the results.

You can know that God is bigger than your inadequacies.

- To be "inadequate" means failing to reach an expected standard, to be insufficient and lacking. God knows all about those things in which we feel insufficient or lacking.

- Sometimes, He leaves us to ourselves so we will recognize how insufficient we are without Him. Then, we'll desire Him more.

ENDURANCE AS YOU VIEW PURPOSE AND REWARD

"For our light and momentary troubles are achieving for us an eternal glory that outweighs them all." (2 Corinthians 4:17)

Truth #1: Endurance is good for us.

Endurance in the Bible means "bearing under." It is holding up a load with staying power and stick-to-it-iveness. Endurance teaches us "staying power" for a long-term burden.

Truth #2: Endurance makes us stronger.

Bible study alone won't develop endurance. Just like load-bearing exercise makes your bones stronger, troubles that challenge your faith do that too.

Truth #3: Endurance is necessary to grow up into maturity.

- In the process of human development, the goal is to grow up into a fully functioning, responsible adult. That involves enduring challenges of life so we will grow into maturity.

- But we don't necessarily desire endurance. We get sidetracked with our comforts and our rights. Without endurance, we become satisfied with immaturity. We have men and women refusing to grow up into maturity—in the workplace, in the home, and in the church. God's goal for us is to be mature and complete. Endurance is His tool to help us reach that goal.

Truth #4: Endurance teaches us to depend on God more than on ourselves.

*"Now it is God who makes both us and you **stand firm** in Christ." (2 Corinthians 1:21)*

God wants us to be able to stand firm in Christ. Going through troubles is God's will for us. He allows things in our lives to challenge us, but His motive is not to trip us up. His motive is not to make us fail. He wants to develop that endurance in us so we can stand firm in Him to get us through "whatever."

DO YOU TRY HANDLING IT ALL FIRST THEN GIVE IT TO GOD?

True or False? "When you can no longer handle it yourself, give it to God."   **FALSE**

The biblical truth is that you are NOT supposed to handle it yourself. You cannot handle it yourself, so rely on God from the get-go. That doesn't mean that God isn't going to use your knowledge and experiences to handle the situation. But you are not to start out doing it on your own first.

REASONS WHY GOD WANTS US TO DEPEND ON HIM MORE THAN ON OURSELVES

- ✓ He can demonstrate His power through our frailty, being jars of clay. (4:7)
- ✓ He keeps us from being crushed when we are burdened. (4:8-9)
- ✓ He reveals Jesus' life in and through us. (4:10)
- ✓ He can keep us from losing heart. (4:16)
- ✓ He renews us inwardly while we outwardly "waste away." (4:16)
- ✓ He gives us an eternal perspective about our "light, momentary troubles." (4:18)
- ✓ He will give us a new resurrection/heavenly body as a reward. (4:14; 5:1; 5:5)
- ✓ Because we must live by faith not by sight. (5:7)
- ✓ We will be with Him when this life ends. (5:8)
- ✓ So we will learn how to live to please Him. (5:9)
- ✓ He rewards us for our earthly lives. (5:10)

Let Jesus satisfy your heart with confidence that you can depend on Him. Then, live each day as a God-dependent woman!

5: Your Life Has Purpose

2 Corinthians 5:11-6:10

For Christ's love compels us, because we are convinced that one died for all, and therefore all died. And he died for all, that those who live should no longer live for themselves but for him who died for them and was raised again. (2 Corinthians 5:14-15)

God has put His "light" treasure in your imperfect, easily broken and bruised body so that He can show His all-surpassing power in you and through you. He chooses to use every weakness of yours to demonstrate His strength when we give it over to Him and rely on Him more than on ourselves.

No one denies that life is hard. But it is full of purpose for you and for those whom you touch with your life. As the Spirit daily renews you from within (4:16), you can choose to view your struggles as Paul did—light and momentary—because you know for certain you have a pain-free, hardship-free, joy-filled forever future in the presence of the Lord Jesus Christ. Seeing the face of Christ will make it all worth it!

Questions to consider this week:

- What does Christ's love compel you to do in your life?
- How is your self-image? Do you see yourself the way God sees you? Or do you tend to allow the baggage of your past to tell you who you are?
- What does it mean to be an ambassador for Christ?

THE GOD-DEPENDENT WOMAN

DAY ONE STUDY—GET THE BIG PICTURE.

Ask the Lord Jesus to teach you through His Word.

Read the Bible passage below (NIV, including verses from the last lesson). Use your own method (colored pencils, lines, shapes) to mark 1) anything that grabs your attention, 2) words you want to understand, and 3) topics you have seen before in this letter. Draw arrows between thoughts that connect. Put a star ✱ next to anything you think relates to dependent living.

5 *6 Therefore we are always confident and know that as long as we are at home in the body we are away from the Lord. 7 For we live by faith, not by sight. 8 We are confident, I say, and would prefer to be away from the body and at home with the Lord. 9 So we make it our goal to please him, whether we are at home in the body or away from it. 10 For we must all appear before the judgment seat of Christ, so that each of us may receive what is due us for the things done while in the body, whether good or bad.*

11 Since, then, we know what it is to fear the Lord, we try to persuade others. What we are is plain to God, and I hope it is also plain to your conscience. 12 We are not trying to commend ourselves to you again, but are giving you an opportunity to take pride in us, so that you can answer those who take pride in what is seen rather than in what is in the heart. 13 If we are "out of our mind," as some say, it is for God; if we are in our right mind, it is for you. 14 For Christ's love compels us, because we are convinced that one died for all, and therefore all died. 15 And he died for all, that those who live should no longer live for themselves but for him who died for them and was raised again.

16 So from now on we regard no one from a worldly point of view. Though we once regarded Christ in this way, we do so no longer. 17 Therefore, if anyone is in Christ, the new creation has come: The old has gone, the new is here! 18 All this is from God, who reconciled us to himself through Christ and gave us the ministry of reconciliation: 19 that God was reconciling the world to himself in Christ, not counting people's sins against them. And he has committed to us the message of reconciliation. 20 We are therefore Christ's ambassadors, as though God were making his appeal through us. We implore you on Christ's behalf: Be reconciled to God. 21 God made him who had no sin to be sin for us, so that in him we might become the righteousness of God.

6 *As God's co-workers we urge you not to receive God's grace in vain. 2 For he says, "In the time of my favor I heard you, and in the day of salvation I helped you." I tell you, now is the time of God's favor, now is the day of salvation.*

3 We put no stumbling block in anyone's path, so that our ministry will not be discredited. 4 Rather, as servants of God we commend ourselves in every way: in great endurance; in troubles, hardships and distresses; 5 in beatings, imprisonments and riots; in hard work, sleepless nights and hunger; 6 in purity, understanding, patience and kindness; in the Holy Spirit and in sincere love; 7 in truthful speech and in the power of God; with weapons of righteousness in the right hand and in the left; 8 through glory and dishonor, bad report and good report; genuine, yet regarded as impostors; 9 known, yet regarded as unknown; dying, and yet we live on; beaten, and yet not killed; 10 sorrowful, yet always rejoicing; poor, yet making many rich; having nothing, and yet possessing everything.

LESSON FIVE

1. What grabbed your attention from these verses?
   - Vv. 11-15

   - vv. 16-21

   - vv. 6:1-10

2. What verses or specific words do you want to understand better?

3. What topics are repeated in this passage or continue an earlier discussion in this letter?

4. What verses illustrate or help you understand what dependent living on God looks like?

Respond to the Lord about what He has shown you today.

THE GOD-DEPENDENT WOMAN

DAY TWO STUDY

Read 2 Corinthians 5:11-15. Ask the Lord Jesus to teach you through His Word.

What does the Bible say?

5. Look carefully at these verses which lead up to the more familiar verses in this chapter.

    Scriptural Insight: Consider that v. 11 follows v. 10—the judgment seat of Christ.

    Because Paul knows what it is to fear (revere) the Lord, what does he do (v. 11)?

    What opportunity is Paul giving to the Corinthians (v. 12)?

    What drives Paul and his team to try to persuade others to believe the gospel (v. 14)?

    How should believers who received the gospel and now "live" respond to Christ's love (v. 15)?

    Did anything else grab your attention?

What does it mean?

6. Transparency is an important virtue in our world as it was back in Paul's day. Compare 5:11 with what Paul has already said in 2 Corinthians 1:12-13 and 4:2. Summarize what he wants them to believe about him.

7. Focus on vv. 12-13. Consider what you read earlier in this letter, and check other translations.
    - What could Paul mean by "taking pride in what is seen rather than in what is in the heart" (v. 12)?

    - The start of verse 13 could be a slander against Paul. How does he respond?

LESSON FIVE

8. Focus on vv. 14-15. What is Paul saying here? How should that look?

> **Focus on the Meaning:** The engine that should drive our spiritual life is the overwhelming gratitude we should feel at the gracious love of God for us. **We are the beloved**. If you are not firmly grounded in that TRUTH, what motives are fueling your spiritual life?

9. What else did you learn as you studied 2 Corinthians 5:11-15?

What application will you make?

10. Paul affirmed that Christ's love compels him to continue preaching the gospel to persuade others to trust the Lord. What does Christ's love compel you to do (v. 14) in your life?

11. How does taking pride in what's seen rather than what's in the heart (v.12) impact our ability to live for Him instead of for ourselves (v.15)?"

12. In what other ways can you apply this lesson to your life?

Respond to the Lord about what He has shown you today.

THE GOD-DEPENDENT WOMAN

Day Three Study

Read 2 Corinthians 5:16-21. Ask the Lord Jesus to teach you through His Word.

What does the Bible say?

13. Complete the following thoughts based on what is written in the biblical text.

    From now on, how do we not regard anyone (v. 16)?

    What is true about anyone who is in Christ (v. 17)?

    All this is from God who (v. 18) _____
      and gave us _____.

    That God was (v. 19) _____
      not counting _____.
      And He has committed to us _____.

    We are (v. 20) _____ as though God
      were _____. We implore you
      on Christ's behalf: _____.

    Write out v. 21 (often called "The Great Exchange") in the space below.

    From the Greek: In v. 17, Paul used the Greek term *ktisis* (translated creature, "creation"). The rabbis used this term referring to someone who converted from idolatry to Judaism. The Corinthians would have been familiar with this term.

What does it mean?

14. Read v. 16 in several Bible translations. Paul's phrase "worldly point of view" (v. 16) literally means "according to the flesh." It refers to the human perspective.

    - How would someone regard Christ from a worldly point of view?

    - How could we regard other people from a worldly point of view?

LESSON FIVE

Scriptural Insight: Before his conversion, Paul had looked at people on a strictly physical basis, in terms of their *ethnicity* rather than their spiritual status—which was the merely human perspective. Now, whether a person was a believer or a non-believer was more important to him than whether he or she was a Jew or a Gentile. Paul had also formerly concluded that Jesus could not be the divine Messiah, in view of His lowly origin, rejection, and humiliating death. Now he recognized (knew) Him for who He really was, and what He really had done. (*Dr. Constable's Notes on 2 Corinthians 2017 Edition,* p. 63)

15. What does Paul mean by "new creation" in v. 17? Draw from what you have learned so far in 2 Corinthians and any other verses that explain this.

Scriptural Insight: At the moment of salvation, every believer is made into something that never existed before then. In God's eyes, you are now fused with Christ (Rom. 6:5), one of God's saints (2 Cor. 1:1), adopted as His child (Rom. 8:16; Gal. 3:26), permanently indwelt by His Spirit (John 14:16-17), and made a member of the Body of Christ (1 Cor. 12:13). Viewing every person as to whether they are in Christ already or needing to be introduced to Him changes our perspective about people (v. 16). And God is committed to the process of changing you (Philippians 1:6; 2:12-13).

16. Focus on vv. 18-20.

- What has God chosen to do in spite of our frailties (vv. 18-20)?

- What is the role of an ambassador? Feel free to look up the definition first.

- What is your message as an ambassador to the world?

Think About It: Recall how Paul talked about having the treasure of the gospel in jars of clay (4:7). The treasure includes the message of reconciliation. You can know and live with confidence that the barrier of sin has been taken away and a bridge has been built between you and God because of Jesus' finished work on the cross. This was God's act of reconciliation offered to you and the reason He is no longer counting your sins against you (v. 20). By believing in His Son, your relationship with God is restored…no longer broken. How does that make you feel?

THE GOD-DEPENDENT WOMAN

17. If God is no longer counting our sins against us (v. 20) so that we can be reconciled to Him, where has our sin gone (v. 21)?

> **Scriptural Insight:** This is the "Great Exchange." When Adam sinned, sin entered the world. Adam's sin brought death, so death spread to everyone, for everyone sinned (Romans 5:12). We sin because we are sinners. At the cross, God made Him who knew no sin (Jesus) to be sin for us so that we could receive His righteousness as our own in place of our sin (2 Corinthians 5:21) forever.

18. What is the one sin that God does count against those who are not Christians? See John 3:16-18; 16:8-9.

> **Scriptural Insight:** One of the Holy Spirit's jobs on earth is to convict people of their sin of unbelief regarding Jesus as the Son of God (John 16:8-9). Those who refuse to respond to the Holy Spirit's leading are not saved. In Mark 3:29, Jesus talks about blasphemy (slander) against the Holy Spirit. Blasphemy against the Holy Spirit is this: "The malicious resistance against the Holy Spirit's converting power after one is shown that Jesus is the Christ." It is like a line in the sand. Those who cross the line by believing in Jesus are saved; those who refuse to cross and believe will be held accountable for their sin of unbelief.

What application will you make?

19. Do you see yourself the way God sees you? Or do you tend to allow the baggage of your past tell you who you are? Can you accept what verse 17 says, that you are a new creation in Christ? How could that change your outlook, your lifestyle, and your relationships?

> **Think About It:** Start using your new identity. See yourself as a righteous, dearly loved holy child of God. Renew your mind according to it. Trust Him to adapt your behavior to align with it (Ephesians 4:1).

20. In what other ways can you apply this lesson to your life?

Respond to the Lord about what He has shown you today.

LESSON FIVE

DAY FOUR STUDY

Read 2 Corinthians 6:1-10. Ask the Lord Jesus to teach you through His Word.

What does the Bible say?

21. Paul gives examples from his own life of what it means to live as an ambassador and a servant of God, including more "light and momentary troubles." He wrote this letter from Macedonia after he left Ephesus. All these events took place before the end of his third missionary journey in Acts 20. See examples of his experiences in Acts 14, 16 and 19.

    As God's co-worker and servant in a time of God's favor, what is Paul's aim in ministry (v. 3)?

    As servants of God, believers commend themselves (and avoid being stumbling blocks) by their responses to daily life and its challenges. Complete the charts below. Circle the challenges that can happen to anyone, not just those being persecuted for their faith.

The challenges (6:4-5)	The responses (6:6-7)

	What is not-so-good	What is good
v. 8		
v. 9		
v. 10		

    Did anything else grab your attention?

    From the Greek: The Greek word translated endurance or perseverance means "bearing under." It is holding up a load with staying power, tenacity and stick-to-it-iveness. It enables a person to stand on his or her feet when facing a storm head on. "Weapons of righteousness" are tools of righteousness—all the godly responses to trouble that Paul stated in 6:6-7. See also Romans 6:13 where it is translated "instruments of righteousness."

THE GOD-DEPENDENT WOMAN

What does it mean?

22. To understand 6:1-3, remember that the context is being an ambassador for Christ and living for Him (5:15-21).

    - As those working together with God, what does Paul urge the Corinthians not to do (v. 1)?

    - How could you receive God's grace in vain in this context? Verse 3 gives a clue.

    - How are the Corinthians allowing themselves to be used as stumbling blocks to others who might be drawn to believe in Christ?

23. Once again, Paul talks about "endurance." In the last lesson, you learned that endurance has purpose and reward.

    - Read Romans 5:3-5. What does endurance or perseverance produce in us (purpose)?

    - What is the evidence for this in 2 Corinthians 6:6-10 (reward)?

24. What else did you learn as you studied 2 Corinthians 6:1-10?

What application will you make?

As Christians, when we encounter stress, pressure, pain and suffering, we are more susceptible to wiggle, run, compromise, or sin to avoid the suffering. Paul wrote to encourage suffering believers to patiently endure, to persevere through the challenges and receive God's comfort in the process (2 Corinthians 1:6).

LESSON FIVE

25. Do you recognize in Paul's experiences any of your own life challenges?

- Choose one and consider your response to that challenge in your life and how you were or were not a good ambassador for Christ during that time.

- What have you learned since that time about trusting Christ that enables you to be an ambassador for Him even during tough times?

> **Dependent Living:** The only way to live this kind of life is by a conscious dependence on God's Spirit.

26. In what other ways can you apply this lesson to your life?

27. Review the passage for this lesson in "Day One Study." Add reasons why God wants us to depend on Him more than on ourselves to the chart below. I have given a few prompts.

Verse(s)	Reasons why God wants us to depend on Him more than on ourselves
5:15	So we can live for Him rather than for ourselves
5:17	He has made us into a new creation
5:19-20	We are His ambassadors and speak for Him
5:21	He exchanges our sin for Christ's righteousness

Respond to the Lord about what He has shown you today.

THE GOD-DEPENDENT WOMAN

As His child, God transforms your life by teaching you to live dependently on Him in weakness and in strength.

Recommended: Listen to "The Gifts of the New Creation, Part 1" to reinforce what you have learned. Use the following listener guide.

LESSON FIVE

PODCAST LISTENER GUIDE

The Gifts of the New Creation, Part 1

As a direct result of Christ's finished work on the cross, our relationship with God is changed because of our faith in Jesus Christ. This change is described by six terms that are sometimes called the "words of the cross." They are gifts we receive as new creations in Christ.

WORD OF THE CROSS #1 IS PROPITIATION. IT MEANS THAT "GOD'S HOLY WRATH AGAINST SIN IS FULLY SATISFIED."

- God's wrath is His decision to preserve His creation by destroying whatever would destroy it—sin and evil. Just like you destroy viruses invading your safe home environment.

- God's wrath is far more serious, of course. Sin is much more awful with far more destructive consequences than the flu virus. Sin hampers our relationship with God. He wanted to do something to restore the relationship.

- Our loving God took action. God presented Christ as a sacrifice of **propitiation** for our sins, a word that means to be appeased, to be satisfied. Therefore, God's holy wrath against all sin is fully satisfied by Jesus' sacrifice on the cross. Because of that, God is able to extend mercy to every believer in Christ. *Romans 3:25; Romans 5:9*

- There is no longer any sacrifice that anyone can ever do to satisfy God's wrath against sin apart from what Christ has already done. It is done, finished!

- Because you have trusted Christ and are now found in Christ, you can know and live with confidence that God is fully **satisfied…no longer angry** at your sin—ever!

WORD OF THE CROSS #2 IS RECONCILIATION. IT MEANS THAT "OUR RELATIONSHIP WITH GOD IS RESTORED."

- All people have sinned and fall short of the glory of God. Before Christ came, we were alienated from God—having a broken relationship with our Creator. *Romans 3:23*

- God restored our broken relationship with Him by reconciling us to Himself through Jesus' death on the cross. It is complete reconciliation, never to be broken again. *Colossians 1:20-22*

- God chose to do that out of His love for us. *Romans 5:10*

- God has given us the ministry of reconciliation to extend His invitation to others. And the same power of reconciliation is available to you through Christ for your relationships with others. *2 Corinthians 5:18-19*

WORD OF THE CROSS #3 IS REDEMPTION. IT MEANS THAT YOU ARE "PURCHASED OUT OF BONDAGE TO SIN AND RELEASED INTO FREEDOM TO SERVE GOD."

- Every human born on this planet is born into bondage to the kingdom of darkness, sin, and the empty way of life we get from human traditions. *Colossians 1:13; 2:8; Romans 6.*

- In Mark 10:45, Jesus declared that He came to give His life as a *ransom* for many—to pay the purchase price out of our slavery to sin with His blood. But more than that, we have been **released into freedom** to serve God with our bodies and souls in obedience to Hm.

- Out of His love and His purpose for us, God rescues us from the dominion of darkness and from all wickedness. He does this to release us to be purified as a people that are His very own, eager to do what is good, and to serve Him as His representative to others. *Colossians 1:13; Titus 2:14*

- He rescues us from this earthly body with sin still assaulting us and releases us at death when He gives us a new, perfect body, fashioned for life in heaven with God. *2 Corinthians 5:1-10*

- Because you have trusted Christ and are now found in Christ, you can know and live with confidence that you are now **released…no longer in bondage** to sin and guilt.

Since you have trusted Christ and are now found in Christ, you can know and live with confidence that your relationship with God is **restored…no longer broken** because of sin.

DO MY HAPPINESS, HEALTH, AND BLESSINGS IN LIFE DEPEND ON OBEDIENCE TO GOD?

True or False? "Your happiness and your health and your blessings in this life depend on your obedience to God!"   **FALSE**

Obedience to God does give us protection from some of the consequences of sin. But if happiness is based on good happenings, obedience does not guarantee that. This is a false teaching, slanted to making you guilty for lack of obedience to God if bad things happen to you.

REASONS WHY GOD WANTS US TO DEPEND ON HIM MORE THAN ON OURSELVES

- ✓ So we can live for Him rather than for ourselves. (5:15)
- ✓ He has made us into a new creation. (5:17)
- ✓ We are His ambassadors and speak for Him. (5:19-20)
- ✓ He exchanges our sin for Christ's righteousness. (5:21)
- ✓ We are His servants. (6:4)
- ✓ So we respond to troubles in a godly manner. (6:4-9)
- ✓ Our lives influence others. (6:10)

Let Jesus satisfy your heart with confidence that you can depend on Him. Then, live each day as a God-dependent woman!

6: Open Wide Your Hearts

2 Corinthians 6:11-7:16

Therefore, since we have these promises, dear friends, let us purify ourselves from everything that contaminates body and spirit, perfecting holiness out of reverence for God. Make room for us in your hearts. We have wronged no one, we have corrupted no one, we have exploited no one. (2 Corinthians 7:1-2)

You are the beloved child of the living God who, in His love, has made you into a new creature with a definite purpose. You are the aroma of the knowledge of God for others to sense. You are a righteous light-bearer of God's glory that shines even in your weakness. You are able to view other people through the lens of their relationship to Christ or need for Him rather than through worldly prejudices. That is who you are, dear Christian, in God's eyes—the only view that really matters.

Yet, our frail bodies live in a world filled with struggles. People around us see how we respond and may be drawn to Christ by watching us live with integrity and sincere dependence on the Lord Jesus. This is also true in our relationships with other believers, as Paul addresses in this next section of his letter. His appeal to the Corinthians who are like family to him may resonate in something you have experienced as well. "Open wide your hearts, as we have opened ours to you."

Questions to consider this week:

- How do you recognize when you are being contaminated in body and spirit by a relationship or activity? What should you do about it?
- What is the difference between godly sorrow and the "I'm sorry" the world practices?

THE GOD-DEPENDENT WOMAN

DAY ONE STUDY—GET THE BIG PICTURE.

Ask the Lord Jesus to teach you through His Word.

Read the Bible passage below (NIV). Use your own method (colored pencils, lines, shapes) to mark 1) anything that grabs your attention, 2) words you want to understand, and 3) topics you have seen before in this letter. Draw arrows between thoughts that connect. Put a star ✱ next to anything you think relates to dependent living.

6 11 We have spoken freely to you, Corinthians, and opened wide our hearts to you. 12 We are not withholding our affection from you, but you are withholding yours from us. 13 As a fair exchange—I speak as to my children—open wide your hearts also.

14 Do not be yoked together with unbelievers. For what do righteousness and wickedness have in common? Or what fellowship can light have with darkness? 15 What harmony is there between Christ and Belial? Or what does a believer have in common with an unbeliever? 16 What agreement is there between the temple of God and idols? For we are the temple of the living God. As God has said:

"I will live with them and walk among them, and I will be their God, and they will be my people."

17 Therefore, "Come out from them and be separate, says the Lord. Touch no unclean thing, and I will receive you."

18 And, "I will be a Father to you, and you will be my sons and daughters, says the Lord Almighty."

7 Therefore, since we have these promises, dear friends, let us purify ourselves from everything that contaminates body and spirit, perfecting holiness out of reverence for God.

2 Make room for us in your hearts. We have wronged no one, we have corrupted no one, we have exploited no one. 3 I do not say this to condemn you; I have said before that you have such a place in our hearts that we would live or die with you. 4 I have spoken to you with great frankness; I take great pride in you. I am greatly encouraged; in all our troubles my joy knows no bounds.

5 For when we came into Macedonia, we had no rest, but we were harassed at every turn—conflicts on the outside, fears within. 6 But God, who comforts the downcast, comforted us by the coming of Titus, 7 and not only by his coming but also by the comfort you had given him. He told us about your longing for me, your deep sorrow, your ardent concern for me, so that my joy was greater than ever.

8 Even if I caused you sorrow by my letter, I do not regret it. Though I did regret it—I see that my letter hurt you, but only for a little while— 9 yet now I am happy, not because you were made sorry, but because your sorrow led you to repentance. For you became sorrowful as God intended and so were not harmed in any way by us. 10 Godly sorrow brings repentance that leads to salvation and leaves no regret, but worldly sorrow brings death. 11 See what this godly sorrow has produced in you: what earnestness, what eagerness to clear yourselves, what indignation, what alarm, what longing, what concern, what readiness to see justice done. At every point you have proved yourselves to be innocent in this matter. 12 So even though I wrote to you, it was neither on account of the one who did the wrong nor on account of the injured party, but rather that before God you could see for yourselves how devoted to us you are. 13 By all this we are encouraged.

In addition to our own encouragement, we were especially delighted to see how happy Titus was, because his spirit has been refreshed by all of you. 14 I had boasted to him about you, and you have not embarrassed me. But just as everything we said to you was true, so our boasting about you to Titus has proved to be true as well. 15 And his affection for you is all the greater when he *remembers that you were all obedient, receiving him with fear and trembling. 16 I am glad I can have complete confidence in you.*

1. What grabbed your attention from these verses?
   - 6:11-7:1

   - 7:2-7

   - 7:8-16

2. What verses or specific words do you want to understand better?

3. What topics are repeated in this passage or continue an earlier discussion in this letter?

4. What verses illustrate or help you understand what dependent living on God looks like?

Respond to the Lord about what He has shown you today.

THE GOD-DEPENDENT WOMAN

DAY TWO STUDY

Read 2 Corinthians 6:11-7:1. Ask the Lord Jesus to teach you through His Word.

What does the Bible say?

5. Paul appeals to their hearts and to their choices that influence their hearts.

   What does Paul declare to the Corinthians (v. 11)?

   Who is withholding affection (v. 12)?

   What does he ask them to do (v. 13)?

   What does he tell them not to do (v. 14)?

   For we are what (v. 16)?

   What has God already said about this "separateness" (v. 17)?

   Since we have the promises in 6:16-18, and are the temple of the living God, what should we do (7:1)?

   Did anything else grab your attention?

   > **Scriptural Insight:** "Belial" (v. 15) is the personification of Evil (cf. Deuteronomy 13:13; 2 Samuel 22:5-6), and he is the antithesis of Christ. "Belial" was a recognized name for "Satan" in Paul's day. It may have come from combining the Hebrew word for "worthlessness" with the name of the pagan god "Baal. (*Dr. Constable's Notes on 2 Corinthians 2017 Edition*, p. 75)

What does it mean?

This section of text summarizes 1 Corinthians 10:1-22, where Paul had previously warned the Corinthians about idolatry. This extended to relationships as well as behavior. Being unequally yoked refers to the disastrous results of yoking a bigger, compliant ox with a smaller, stubborn donkey together (Deuteronomy 22:10). Did you notice all the contrasts Paul used? Righteousness / wickedness; light / darkness; Christ / Belial; believer / unbeliever; and the temple of God / idols.

LESSON SIX

He is also used descriptive joining words: have in common, fellowship, harmony, and agreement. The word pictures Paul painted should help us to understand what he means.

6. Read vv. 14-16 in several Bible translations then answer the following questions. From the original language, we learn that Paul is addressing individual believers. But we know that individuals by their choices influence the whole community.

- What would be the general answer to all five questions that Paul asks?

- What could it mean to be yoked together with unbelievers?

- In what situations / relationships do you think this teaching against being "yoked together with unbelievers" especially applies?

- What is the difference between being "yoked together" and being a "bridge-builder" as an ambassador for Christ?

- How could being yoked together with unbelievers be detrimental to you as a believer? Look throughout today's passage for your answer.

- What should you do to prevent yourself from being unequally yoked?

> **Scriptural Insight:** Paul was not saying that Christians should break off all association with unbelievers (cf. 1 Corinthians 5:9-10; 10:27). He had previously encouraged the saved partner in a mixed marriage to maintain the marriage relationship as long as possible (1 Corinthians 7:12-16). He had also urged his fellow Christians, as ambassadors of Christ, to evangelize the lost (2 Corinthians 5:20). Rather, here Paul was commanding that Christians form no binding interpersonal relationships with non-Christians *that resulted in their spiritual defilement*. ... Such alliances can prevent the Christian from living a consistently obedient Christian life. (*Dr. Constable's Notes on 2 Corinthians 2017 Edition*, p. 74)

THE GOD-DEPENDENT WOMAN

7. Every Christian is the temple of the living God. What makes us the temple of God? See also 2 Corinthians 1:22, 5:5 and 6:19-20.

8. What else did you learn as you studied 2 Corinthians 6:11-7:1?

What application will you make?

9. **Broken relationships:** Paul talks about the pain of broken relationships in 6:11-13. Is this something you are experiencing within your family or with friends? Paul gets it. Jesus gets it. It hurts. How can you follow the process Paul gives throughout 2 Corinthians 6:11-7:16?

10. **Contaminating relationships:** Review 2 Corinthians 7:1. To purify yourself from everything that contaminates body and spirit means to separate yourself from ungodly, immoral, and reputation-ruining activities.

    - How do you recognize when you are being contaminated in body and spirit by a relationship or activity?

    - What should you do to keep from being contaminated by that relationship or activity?

    Scriptural Insight: What if you are married to an unbeliever? See 1 Peter 3 and 1 Corinthians 7. What if you work for an unbeliever or are in business with an unbeliever? See Colossians 3. What if your adult children are unbelievers? See Luke 15. Be careful about causes that you support. See Acts 13:50 and Galatians 6:10.

LESSON SIX

11. In what other ways can you apply this lesson to your life?

> **Think About It:** Flee, don't flirt with corrupting influences of the secular culture. Flirting with it would be considering, "How close can I get to the line of sin without crossing over?" Fleeing from it would be "How far away can I get from the line of sin so I am not close enough to cross over?" (Destin Garner, RockPointe Church sermon, June 25, 2017). We often put more effort into being "anti-germ" than we do in being "anti-sin." Consider the corrupting influences from the secular culture to be as dangerous to your health as the presence of germs in your space.

Respond to the Lord about what He has shown you today.

DAY THREE STUDY

Read 2 Corinthians 7:2-7. Ask the Lord Jesus to teach you through His Word.

What does the Bible say?

12. Review 2 Corinthians 2:12-13 to remember the situation that Paul is addressing. Paul picks up on his wording from 6:11-13.

    Paul asked them to do what (v. 2)?

    Paul declares that no one had been _____, _____,
    and _____ by him (v. 2).

    What had Paul said before (v. 3)?

    What did Paul tell them (v. 4)?

    When Paul and his friends came into Macedonia, what did they experience (v. 5)?

    But God does what (v. 6)?

THE GOD-DEPENDENT WOMAN

The Corinthians had given comfort to Titus who told Paul what (v. 7)?

Paul's response was what (v. 7)?

Did anything else grab your attention?

What does it mean?

13. Review 7:2-4. Paul is baring his heart to the Corinthian Christians. Summarize what Paul is saying.

14. God brings comfort to Paul's anxious heart concerning the Corinthians (vv. 5-7; 2:1-4). The context is relationship concerns.

    - Why did Paul need comfort?

    - What did God use to comfort him?

    - How did this comforting news affect Paul?

    > **From the Greek:** Paul had felt *disheartened* (Gr. *tapeinos*, meaning "brought low, humble, lowly in spirit," not clinically "depressed") when he could not find Titus as he first arrived in Macedonia. He was so concerned about how the Corinthians had received his severe letter that he couldn't rest until he heard the news. This is not despair which means you feel hopeless (2 Corinthians 4:2). A Christian is never hopeless!

15. What else did you learn as you studied 2 Corinthians 7:2-7?

LESSON SIX

What application will you make?

16. Recall a time when you felt disheartened or downcast, and God sent others to encourage and lift you up. Have you recognized that comfort being from Him? _____ Have you thanked Him for it? _____

Respond to the Lord about what He has shown you today.

Day Four Study

Read 2 Corinthians 7:8-16. Ask the Lord Jesus to teach you through His Word.

What does the Bible say?

17. In 2 Corinthians 7:8-16, Paul returns to his train of thought from earlier in the letter. Review 2 Corinthians 2:1-11.

    How does Paul feel about the letter he had to write to them (7:8)?

    Why is he now happy (7:9)?

    Write out 2 Corinthians 7:10 below:

    What had godly sorry produced in them (7:11)?

    What had they proven by their response (7:11)?

    What were the reasons he wrote the letter (v. 12)?

93

Besides Paul and Timothy, why was Titus happy (v. 13)?

What proved to be true (v. 14)?

What was Titus's "take-away" from his visit with the Corinthians (v. 15)?

Why is Paul glad (vv. 13, 16)?

Did anything else grab your attention?

> **Think About It:** To reconcile a relationship, one must take deliberate actions and address the problem that caused the breach. These actions hurt but are necessary. Hoping that the misunderstandings will go away on their own rarely works.

What does it mean?

18. Regarding repentance and sorrow for sin (vv. 8-12):
    - Describe godly sorrow from these verses.

    - What could Paul have meant by "worldly sorrow" (v. 10)? Feel free to read this verse in other Bible translations to help in your understanding.

    - What is the difference in outcome and results?

19. What was Titus's role in reconciling the relationship between Paul and the Corinthian church members (vv. 13-16)?

Focus on the Meaning: "Fear and trembling" (v. 15) is likely a *hendiadys*, an idiom in which a verb is intensified by being linked by "and" to a synonym. We have them in English too. If you're "sick and tired," this doesn't mean you're sick *and* you're tired, it just means that you're *very tired*. Similarly, "fear and trembling" seems to mean "great reverence" (or humility) as Paul is using it in 1 Corinthians 2:3; 2 Corinthians 7:15; Philippians 2:12; and Ephesians 6:5. Mark also used this in reference to the woman coming to Jesus in Mark 5:33. The same phrase is found in the Septuagint version of Psalm 2:11 and 55:5. It is the opposite of boasting. (adapted from a posting at Biblical Hermeneutics Stack Exchange)

20. What else did you learn as you studied 2 Corinthians 7:8-16?

What application will you make?

As long as you live in your earthly body, you will be tempted to sin. Sin will happen—whether intentionally or unintentionally. Though our God is no longer counting our sins against us (2 Corinthians 5:20), we still must deal with the consequences of any sinful behavior.

21. Addressing recognized sin in your life is part of dependent living. Whenever the Spirit convicts you of thinking or behavior that is definitely not pleasing to the Lord (2 Corinthians 5:9), follow this biblical process to deal with it:

    - **Step One: View yourself rightly.** Your identity is not "_____" (coveter, greedy, gossiper, whatever it is). You are in Christ, a child of God, who sometimes "_____" (covets, is greedy, gossips).

    - **Step Two: Recognize (confess) the truth regarding your sin.** To confess biblically means *to agree with God about what you and He both know to be true*. Confession is not a formula, a process, or dependent on a mediator. Regarding sin in my life, it is not saying, "I'm sorry." It is saying, "I agree with you, God. I blew it!" See your sin as awful!

      Using coveting for example: while reading Philippians 4:12, the Spirit convicts you that you have been coveting rather than being content. You agree with God that your coveting is actually not being content with His provision. Coveting doesn't fit someone who knows God. That is confession.

    - **Step Three: Confession is incomplete without repentance.** Repentance means *to change your mind about that sin, to mourn its ugliness, resulting in changing your actions.* Paul calls that godly sorrow in 2 Corinthians 7:9-11, and he says godly sorrow produces repentance. It is saying, "I recognize what I am doing is wrong. This fills me with sorrow because it displeases You, God. Please help me to live differently." He will certainly do that! God uses sorrow over sin to get His desired results. That is how our lives get transformed.

      Using coveting for example: You want to not covet any longer, and you want to be content and grateful for what God has already provided. So, you pray, "Lord Jesus, please have your Spirit nudge me when I want to covet. Replace my coveting with contentment and gratitude. By faith, Lord, I want you to do that in my life." That is repentance.

- **Step Four: Repentance leads to dependence.** Depend on the living Christ inside you for that change to take place. Our Lord Jesus Christ is not interested in our compliance (outward conformity) as much as He desires our *obedience* from the heart. And trust in Him to help you overcome the consequences of any sinful choices you have made in a way that brings glory to Him.

    Using coveting for example: Memorize Philippians 4:12-13 and any other scriptures that deal with being thankful for God's provision. Be sensitive to the Spirit's nudging when you are tempted to covet. Choose to be thankful instead.

> **Think About It:** Repentance isn't repentance until you change something. You can confess "until the cows come home" (daily, habitually) and never change anything. Jesus called for people to "repent" not "confess."

22. In what other ways can you apply this lesson to your life?

23. Review the passage for this lesson in "Day One Study." Add reasons why God wants us to depend on Him more than on ourselves to the chart below. I have given a few prompts.

Verse(s)	Reasons why God wants us to depend on Him more than on ourselves
6:16-18	We are His children
7:1	To purify ourselves to perfect holiness
7:6	He comforts us when we are downcast
7:9	So we rightly respond to sin in our lives

Respond to the Lord about what He has shown you today.

LESSON SIX

As His child, God transforms your life by teaching you to live dependently on Him in weakness and in strength.

> **Recommended:** Listen to "The Gifts of the New Creation, Part 2" to reinforce what you have learned. Use the following listener guide.

The Gifts of the New Creation, Part 2

As a direct result of Christ's finished work on the cross, our relationship with God is changed because of our faith in Jesus Christ. This change is described by six terms that are sometimes called the "words of the cross." They are gifts we receive as new creations in Christ.

WORD OF THE CROSS #4 IS FORGIVENESS. IT MEANS THAT "YOUR GUILT HAS BEEN TAKEN AWAY."

- We can carry our baggage as a burden. God stepped in and did for us what we couldn't do for ourselves. He transferred our sin to a substitute, Jesus, and it was taken away.

    *"When you were dead in your sins…God made you alive with Christ. He forgave us **all** our sins, having canceled the charge of our legal indebtedness, which stood against us and condemned us; He has **taken it away**, nailing it to the cross." (Colossians 2:13-14)*

- Once you trust in Jesus Christ, what you have done wrong in God's eyes from the time you were born through the time of your death has been canceled. Past, present and future. He is no longer counting our sins against us. *2 Corinthians 5:19*

- As long as you live in your earthly body, you will sometimes sin. As an already forgiven Christian, the biblical process for dealing with recognized sin is to remember first that your identity is child of God, agree with God that you have sinned against Him, mourn your sin and depend on the Holy Spirit to help you obey God in the future. Then, trust in Him to help you overcome the consequences of any sinful choices you have made in a way that brings glory to Him. That is living a life that pleases the Lord in every way.

- Because you have trusted Christ and are now found in Christ, you can know and live with confidence that you have been **forgiven…no longer burdened** by your sin and guilt. Allow Jesus to cleanse your conscience from any residual guilt.

WORD OF THE CROSS #5 IS JUSTIFICATION. IT MEANS THAT "YOU ARE DECLARED RIGHTEOUS IN GOD'S EYES."

- There are two aspects to justification. The first aspect is the removal of guilt from the offender. That is forgiveness. The second aspect is the addition of righteousness to the one who believes. That is justification. The two aspects together are called the "Great Exchange." *2 Corinthians 5:21*

- The amazing thing is that God does this while we are still capable of sinning! When God looks on you, He sees His Son's righteousness taking the place of your sin—even your sin after you have been a believer for a long time.

- When you are tempted to think that God could not possibly accept you because of your weaknesses and guilty past, declare this to yourself: "Because of my faith in Jesus Christ, I am declared **righteous…no longer guilty** in God's sight." That is a fact.

LESSON SIX

WORD OF THE CROSS #6 IS SANCTIFICATION. IT MEANS TO BE "SET APART AS GOD'S POSSESSION FOR HIS EXCLUSIVE USE."

- God is the ultimate perfectionist. God determines what He considers good. None of our little checklists measure up. The only human who was ever good enough for God was Jesus.

- To be sanctified means to be made holy—to be "set apart from anything evil." By faith in Jesus Christ, God declares us holy in His sight. We are clothed with Christ (Galatians 3:27). When God looks on you and me, He sees Jesus and His righteousness, not all of our faults. His love chooses to do that for us.

- You have been set apart as God's special, beloved possession for His exclusive use, called by Him to be dedicated to His service—a purpose.

- You are also "being made holy" in your thoughts, words, and actions by the work of the Holy Spirit. This is ongoing from the moment of salvation until the Lord comes or you die, when your "being made holy" is complete. We make choices that reflect our desire to set ourselves apart from sin and to God's purposes for us. *2 Corinthians 7:1*

- Because you have trusted in Christ and are now found in Him, you can know and live with confidence that you are set apart by God, for God. In His sight, you are **perfected...no longer flawed.** Your behavior matches this status when you submit to the Spirit's work.

- We should respond to all His gifts with love for Him and gratitude for what He has done in our lives.

DOES GOD GIVE THE HARDEST BATTLES TO HIS STRONGEST SOLDIERS?

True or False? "When you are having a rough time, just remember that God gives the hardest battles to His strongest soldiers." **FALSE**

Going back to what we've learned in 2 Corinthians so far, we are all jars of clay. Weak. Frail. God puts His treasure, Himself, in all of us because we are all weak, and He wants us to know that any power to fight a battle is from God and not from us. Our strength comes from being clothed in Christ not as wonder woman.

REASONS WHY GOD WANTS US TO DEPEND ON HIM MORE THAN ON OURSELVES

- ✓ We are His children. (6:16-18)
- ✓ To purify ourselves to perfect holiness. (7:1)
- ✓ He comforts us when we are downcast. (7:6)
- ✓ So we rightly respond to sin in our lives. (7:9)
- ✓ To see truth in ourselves, in our hearts. (7:12)

Let Jesus satisfy your heart with confidence that you can depend on Him. Then, live each day as a God-dependent woman!

> LESSON SEVEN

7: Generosity from Joy Overflowing

2 Corinthians 8:1-9:15

And now, brothers and sisters, we want you to know about the grace that God has given the Macedonian churches. In the midst of a very severe trial, their overflowing joy and their extreme poverty welled up in rich generosity. (2 Corinthians 8:1-2)

Paul's heart was hurting because the Corinthian Christians closed off their affection for him. The relationship was broken, at least temporarily, for several reasons—misunderstandings, slander against him, and his need to send them a stern letter warning them about their sinful behavior. Paul took deliberate steps to address the problems. He was rewarded with comforting words sent by the Corinthians to Paul through Titus. Paul writes that this comfort came from God, and hearing how much they longed for him and were concerned for him made his heart overflow with joy. He saw the fruit of the letter that had needed to be written, though painful for both the writer and the receiver.

To reconcile a relationship, one must take deliberate actions and address the problem that caused the breach. These actions hurt but are necessary. Hoping that the misunderstandings will go away on their own rarely works. The same is true of recognized sin in one's life. You must take deliberate actions that are biblical and lead you to depend on the Lord Jesus Christ even more to overcome whatever that sin is. That also makes your joy overflow as you trust in Him to work in your life.

Now, we come to one of the most amazing passages in the Bible. Paul writes about generosity that springs from overflowing joy, even in the midst of extreme poverty. This is so totally opposite of what the world teaches about money. In Matthew 6:32-33, Jesus told His followers to think differently regarding God's provision. Don't let your needs dominate your thoughts. Your heavenly Father knows them. He cares for the creatures in the natural world so they lack nothing. He will care for you. Give yourself to the Lord first. Pursue what matters to God—His honor and His purposes—more than your own. God's provision to us is not only for our needs but also for us to use to advance His purposes as we are ambassadors for Him. Let's see what that looks like.

Questions to consider this week:

- What is your concept of generosity?
- How do you choose someone trustworthy to handle money for a church community or small group?
- If you are active in ministry to others, do you surround yourself with people worthy of respect who will be trusted by others and, therefore, show you to be trustworthy also?

THE GOD-DEPENDENT WOMAN

DAY ONE STUDY—GET THE BIG PICTURE.

Ask the Lord Jesus to teach you through His Word.

Read the Bible passage below (NIV). Use your own method (colored pencils, lines, shapes) to mark 1) anything that grabs your attention, 2) words you want to understand, and 3) topics you have seen before in this letter. Draw arrows between thoughts that connect. Put a star ✱ next to anything you think relates to dependent living.

> Note: The financial gift is for the impoverished Christians in Jerusalem and Judea.

8 And now, brothers and sisters, we want you to know about the grace that God has given the Macedonian churches. 2 In the midst of a very severe trial, their overflowing joy and their extreme poverty welled up in rich generosity. 3 For I testify that they gave as much as they were able, and even beyond their ability. Entirely on their own, 4 they urgently pleaded with us for the privilege of sharing in this service to the Lord's people. 5 And they exceeded our expectations: They gave themselves first of all to the Lord, and then by the will of God also to us. 6 So we urged Titus, just as he had earlier made a beginning, to bring also to completion this act of grace on your part. 7 But since you excel in everything—in faith, in speech, in knowledge, in complete earnestness and in the love we have kindled in you—see that you also excel in this grace of giving.

8 I am not commanding you, but I want to test the sincerity of your love by comparing it with the earnestness of others. 9 For you know the grace of our Lord Jesus Christ, that though he was rich, yet for your sake he became poor, so that you through his poverty might become rich.

10 And here is my judgment about what is best for you in this matter. Last year you were the first not only to give but also to have the desire to do so. 11 Now finish the work, so that your eager willingness to do it may be matched by your completion of it, according to your means. 12 For if the willingness is there, the gift is acceptable according to what one has, not according to what one does not have.

13 Our desire is not that others might be relieved while you are hard pressed, but that there might be equality. 14 At the present time your plenty will supply what they need, so that in turn their plenty will supply what you need. The goal is equality, 15 as it is written: "The one who gathered much did not have too much, and the one who gathered little did not have too little

16 Thanks be to God, who put into the heart of Titus the same concern I have for you. 17 For Titus not only welcomed our appeal, but he is coming to you with much enthusiasm and on his own initiative. 18 And we are sending along with him the brother who is praised by all the churches for his service to the gospel. 19 What is more, he was chosen by the churches to accompany us as we carry the offering, which we administer in order to honor the Lord himself and to show our eagerness to help. 20 We want to avoid any criticism of the way we administer this liberal gift. 21 For we are taking pains to do what is right, not only in the eyes of the Lord but also in the eyes of man.

22 In addition, we are sending with them our brother who has often proved to us in many ways that he is zealous, and now even more so because of his great confidence in you. 23 As for Titus, he is my partner and co-worker among you; as for our brothers, they are representatives of the churches and an honor to Christ. 24 Therefore show these men the proof of your love and the reason for our pride in you, so that the churches can see it.

9 There is no need for me to write to you about this service to the Lord's people. 2 For I know your eagerness to help, and I have been boasting about it to the Macedonians, telling them that since last year you in Achaia were ready to give; and your enthusiasm has stirred most of them

LESSON SEVEN

to action. 3 But I am sending the brothers in order that our boasting about you in this matter should not prove hollow, but that you may be ready, as I said you would be. 4 For if any Macedonians come with me and find you unprepared, we—not to say anything about you—would be ashamed of having been so confident. 5 So I thought it necessary to urge the brothers to visit you in advance and finish the arrangements for the generous gift you had promised. Then it will be ready as a generous gift, not as one grudgingly given.

6 Remember this: Whoever sows sparingly will also reap sparingly, and whoever sows generously will also reap generously. 7 Each of you should give what you have decided in your heart to give, not reluctantly or under compulsion, for God loves a cheerful giver. 8 And God is able to bless you abundantly, so that in all things at all times, having all that you need, you will abound in every good work. 9 As it is written: "They have freely scattered their gifts to the poor; their righteousness endures forever."

10 Now he who supplies seed to the sower and bread for food will also supply and increase your store of seed and will enlarge the harvest of your righteousness. 11 You will be enriched in every way so that you can be generous on every occasion, and through us your generosity will result in thanksgiving to God.

12 This service that you perform is not only supplying the needs of the Lord's people but is also overflowing in many expressions of thanks to God. 13 Because of the service by which you have proved yourselves, others will praise God for the obedience that accompanies your confession of the gospel of Christ, and for your generosity in sharing with them and with everyone else. 14 And in their prayers for you their hearts will go out to you, because of the surpassing grace God has given you. 15 Thanks be to God for his indescribable gift!

1. What grabbed your attention from these verses?

    - 8:1-9

    - 8:10-24

    - 9:1-15

2. What verses or specific words do you want to understand better?

3. What topics are repeated in this passage or continue an earlier discussion in this letter?

4. What verses illustrate or help you understand what dependent living on God looks like?

Respond to the Lord about what He has shown you today.

DAY TWO STUDY

Read 2 Corinthians 8:1-10. Ask the Lord Jesus to teach you through His Word.

What does the Bible say?

5. God's grace not only saves us but also teaches us to trust Him more and more with our lives and everything we hold dear. Paul is with the Macedonians as he writes this.

   What does Paul want the Corinthians to know (v. 1)?

   Write verse 2 below.

   Who gave the Macedonians the ability to do that?

   Paul testifies what about the Macedonians (v. 3)?

   Entirely on their own, what did they do (v. 4)?

   By what process did they do this (v. 5)? See also Matthew 6:33.

LESSON SEVEN

What was Titus urged to do in Corinth (v. 6)?

In what did the Corinthians already excel (v. 7)?

What did Paul then challenge the Corinthians to do (v. 7)?

What is being tested in their hearts and how (v. 8)?

How did Jesus model the grace of giving for them (v. 9)?

Did anything else grab your attention?

What does it mean?
6. I have given you verse 2 from the NIV in the chart below. Write verse 2 from any three other Bible translations.

NIV	*In the midst of a very severe trial, their overflowing joy and their extreme poverty welled up in rich generosity.*

What is so amazing about what is revealed in verse 2?

Think About It: While undergoing severe trials, afflictions, and extreme poverty, overflowing joy yielded rich generosity. What counts as "rich generosity?" R. G. LeTourneau, who created the first massive earth-moving machines, would often quote this little poem, "It is not what you'd do with a million, if riches should ever be your lot. But what you are doing at present with the dollar and a quarter you've got." So true!

7. Looking at vv. 1-5, identify the choices the Macedonians made in their process of giving. Note: Paul never mentioned the size of their gift.

8. God had gifted the Corinthians with every spiritual gift they needed (1 Corinthians 1:5-7). And Corinth was a prosperous community. They lacked nothing from God.

    - Considering the meaning of grace to be "a gift that is not deserved," what does Paul mean by "this grace of giving (NIV)" / "act of grace (ESV)" in v. 7? What is it not?

    - So, whom are they mimicking in their giving? See also Philippians 2:5-7; 4:19; and Ephesians 1:14, 18.

Scriptural Insight: The incarnation of Jesus Christ is the greatest example of self-sacrificing generosity. He gave up the riches of glory in heaven, when He became a man and died on the cross, so that we might share His riches of glory in heaven (cf. Philippians 2:1-11). Gratitude to Him for His condescending grace should be the supreme motive for Christian giving. ... The Macedonians gave when they were very poor, but Christ gave when He was immensely rich. The Corinthians were between these two extremes. These two examples leave no question that giving is a grace which both the rich and the poor should manifest. (*Dr. Constable's Notes on 2 Corinthians 2017 Edition*, p. 86)

9. Usually, we think of comparison as a bad thing. For what purpose can comparison be good (v. 8)?

LESSON SEVEN

10. What else did you learn as you studied 2 Corinthians 8:1-9?

You might ask, "Where does tithing fit with this grace of giving?" Consider this answer to that question.

> **Scriptural Insight:** Tithing is an Old Testament concept. After the death of Jesus Christ fulfilled the Law, the New Testament nowhere commands, or even recommends, that Christians set aside a certain percentage of income, but only says gifts should be "in keeping with income" (1 Corinthians 16:2). The New Testament talks about giving as we are able. Sometimes that means giving more than 10 percent; sometimes that may mean giving less. It all depends on the ability of the Christian and the needs of the body of Christ. Every Christian should diligently pray and seek God's wisdom in the matter of participating in giving and/or how much to give (2 Corinthians 8:5). Above all, all offerings should be given with pure motives and an attitude of worship to God and service to the body of Christ. "Each man should give what he has decided in his heart to give, not reluctantly or under compulsion, for God loves a cheerful giver" (2 Corinthians 9:7). (*"What does the Bible say about Christian tithing?" from Gotquestions.org*)

What application will you make?

11. What choices must you make to apply this passage to your life? See also Paul's teaching in 1 Corinthians 16:2.

Respond to the Lord about what He has shown you today.

THE GOD-DEPENDENT WOMAN

Day Three Study

Read 2 Corinthians 8:10-24. Ask the Lord Jesus to teach you through His Word.

What does the Bible say?

12. Remember that the context is offering to help the believers in Jerusalem and Judea who are suffering persecution and hardship. In his previous letter, Paul proposed how to make this collection. Read 1 Corinthians 16:1-4. Answer the following questions based on 2 Corinthians 8:10-24.

    Paul reminded them that the Corinthians were the first to do what (v. 10)? See also 9:2.

    Now what should they do (v. 11)?

    What is true if the "willingness is there" (v. 12)?

    What is Paul's desire in encouraging them to give (v. 13)?

    What does Paul state in verse 14?

    ✸Why does Paul thank God (v. 16)?

    What does Paul say about Titus (vv. 17, 23)?

    What does Paul say about the other two men (vv. 18-19, 22)?

    What is Paul being careful to do concerning the offering (vv. 20-21)?

    Did anything else grab your attention?

    > **Scriptural Insight:** Some think "the brother" was Trophimus the Ephesian (Acts 21:29). The other brother may have been one of those mentioned in Acts 20:1-5. All three of them (v. 23) were representatives of the churches and an honor to Christ.

LESSON SEVEN

What does it mean?

Based on v. 10, it's okay to give advice. God gives us a brain to use in making decisions, giving wise counsel, and helping others to see what is best to do in light of the truth of His Word. Paul does that in these verses.

13. Discuss vv. 10-12 regarding the relationship between willingness and intentional action in giving. See also 1 Corinthians 16:2.

14. Examine the sharing principle in verses 13-15. To help in understanding, read these verses in other translations, including "The Message."

    - How is Paul's teaching about equality in provision for Christians in the body of Christ different from the forced equality of socialism?

    - Why is this sharing principle good for the body of Christ? Look at 2 Corinthians 8:1-15 for your answer.

    Scriptural Insight: Paul viewed Christians as being brothers and sisters in a large family. As a family, we have a responsibility to care for each other. ... Paul did not legislate equality; he appealed for it. (*Dr. Constable's Notes on 2 Corinthians 2017 Edition*, p. 87)

15. What wisdom does Paul share in in vv. 19-21 regarding the handling of money belonging to others?

16. What else did you learn as you studied 2 Corinthians 8:10-24?

THE GOD-DEPENDENT WOMAN

What application will you make?

17. Giving is a part of a Christian's faith walk with God. Read 2 Corinthians 8:10-11 in The Message version. What decisions must you make to move from having good intentions to being intentional when it comes to giving?

> **Historical Insight:** The Corinthians did follow through and assemble their gift. It was only a few months after Paul penned 2 Corinthians that he wrote Romans. In that epistle, he said that the Christians of "Macedonia and Achaia" (which includes Corinth) had made a contribution to the poor saints in Jerusalem (Rom. 15:26-27). Paul and his delegation then traveled back to Jerusalem, from Corinth, through Macedonia and Asia Minor (Acts 20:3—21:19). The leaders of the Jerusalem church evidently received the gift gladly (Acts 21:17). (*Dr. Constable's Notes on 2 Corinthians 2017 Edition,* p. 97)

18. From vv. 18-23, we see that it is important to surround yourself in ministry with people worthy of respect who will be trusted by others and therefore show you to be trustworthy, also. What has been your experience in this?

19. In what other ways can you apply this lesson to your life?

Respond to the Lord about what He has shown you today.

Lesson Seven

Day Four Study

Read 2 Corinthians 9:1-15. Ask the Lord Jesus to teach you through His Word.

What does the Bible say?

20. Paul continues his discussion of the grace of giving. Remember, he is with the Macedonians still.

    What compliment does he give in v. 2?

    Why is Paul sending "the brothers" (vv. 3-5)?

    What does he say they need to remember in v. 6 (likely a familiar proverb of the day)?

    How should each person decide what to give (v. 7)?

    What does God love (v. 7)?

    What is God able to do (vv. 8, 10)?

    Why does God give to us (vv. 10-11)?

    What are the benefits of giving generously according to…

    v. 12?

    v. 13?

    v. 14?

    How does Paul conclude this section (v. 15)?

    Did anything else grab your attention?

THE GOD-DEPENDENT WOMAN

> **From the Greek:** We read in 2 Corinthians 9:8 that God is "able to bless you abundantly." That word "bless" (NIV) is from the Greek word *charis*, meaning grace (see 2 Corinthians 1:11 "gracious favor"). Most translations say that God is able to make all grace overflow or abound to you. It refers to His lovingkindness and favor given to you, which may include material provision but is not guaranteeing financial abundance.

What does it mean?

21. ✸ God is the source of all physical and spiritual resources.

    - How does God increase our resources (v. 10)? What does "seed to the sower" mean?

    - Why does God increase our resources (vv. 11-14)?

    > **Think About It:** God gives to us. We give to others. Needs are met. Thanks is given. The gospel is proven to be true. God gets praised. Unity and love increases in the church community and body of Christ as a whole. Sounds like a win/win.

22. What is God's indescribable gift (v. 15)? See 2 Corinthians 8:9; 9:13-14; Ephesians 2:8-9; and John 3:16.

    > **Scriptural Insight:** God is the first giver; He first selflessly gives Himself to us in the person of His Son, and all true Christian giving is our response of gratitude for this gift that is beyond description. See also 1 John 4:9-11. (*NIV Study Bible,* note on v. 15, p. 1773)

23. What else did you learn as you studied 2 Corinthians 9:1-15?

What application will you make?

24. Like those Macedonian Christians, you can ask God to help you determine something you can and will live without for a period of time. Your choice. No one's looking. Take the money you would have spent on that and look for ways to further God's kingdom with it. Or remember a time in your life when God provided what you needed through others giving to meet your needs. It is all His anyway. Give Him the glory.

LESSON SEVEN

25. In what other ways can you apply this lesson to your life?

26. Review the passage for this lesson in "Day One Study." Add reasons why God wants us to depend on Him more than on ourselves to the chart below. I have given a few prompts.

Verse(s)	Reasons why God wants us to depend on Him more than on ourselves
8:1	He initiates the grace of giving
8:5	We need Him to direct our giving according to His will
8:9	He makes us spiritually rich so we can give
8:16	He puts into our hearts concerns for us to have

Respond to the Lord about what He has shown you today.

As His child, God transforms your life by teaching you to live dependently on Him in weakness and in strength.

Recommended: Listen to "Trusting God's Purposes for His Provision" to reinforce what you have learned. Use the following listener guide.

PODCAST LISTENER GUIDE

Trusting God's Purposes for His Provision

At the end of Matthew chapter 6, Jesus told His followers, "Don't let your needs dominate your thoughts." Regarding God's provision, Jesus basically said Christians should **think differently**. Here are four lessons for us to learn.

LESSON #1: GOD'S PROVISION IS HIS TO GIVE AND TAKE AWAY. REGARD IT HUMBLY.

Fact: Everything we have comes from God.

- There isn't anything we have that we did not receive from God. *1 Corinthians 4:7*

- Yet, we humans boastfully live as though we had anything to do with our genetics or privileges at all. When they are stripped away, we resent being stripped of our "rights."

Fact: What we have is not a measure of our goodness or our faith.

- How God chooses to provide for you or me at any time in our lives is His sovereign choice. We are to give ourselves first to Him and trust Him with our daily needs as we do the work He gives us to do. *Philippians 4:12-13; 2 Corinthians 8:7*

  "God is in the human development business. How is God going to teach us faith if He never allows us to have needs?!"

- God's method of learning is to prepare by instruction (knowing His Word) and then to learn by experience (living out what you believe about God). Having needs is part of God's plan. Don't let anyone deceive you by equating prosperity with your faith walk.

- When God removes our comforts and strips away our support, we cry "help," give up our self-sufficiency, and actually begin to depend on God and think of Him as God Almighty—as an essential to our lives, not just an appendage.

Fact: God determines our provision—the how, when, and why

- Most of the time, God's provision is going to come through people, not miraculously appear from the sky. God chooses how He provides for His own. We must learn to trust whatever manner He chooses.

Fact: It belongs to God. Hold onto it loosely.

It is His to give and take away.

LESSON #2: GOD'S PROVISION IS ALWAYS ENOUGH. RECEIVE IT GRATEFULLY.

According to the dictionary, "enough" is "as much as is needed or can be tolerated." I think I can tolerate quite a bit, don't you? But maybe God knows better. I have learned two things about God's enough: it is sufficient, and it can also be very creative.

- The sufficiency of God's enough—When you have the Lord's provision, you lack nothing that you need at this time in your life. It is what you have, not what you don't have. Rejoice at what you have instead of complaining about what you don't have. *Deuteronomy 2:7; Deuteronomy 8:7-9a; 2 Corinthians 6:10*

- The creativity of God's enough—God doesn't do the same thing for everyone.

LESSON #3: GOD'S PROVISION IS MEANT TO BE SHARED. GIVE IT GENEROUSLY.

- Out of the most severe trial, the Macedonian churches' overflowing joy and their extreme poverty welled up in rich generosity. They gave themselves first to the Lord in keeping with God's will. *2 Corinthians 8:1-5*

- They imitated God's generosity and compassion. Compassion requires trusting God, not having plenty. How you handle whatever provision God gives you is very telling.

  It is not what you'd do with a million, if riches should ever be your lot. But what you are doing at present with the dollar and a quarter you've got. (R. G. LeTourneau)

- God's riches to us are supplied through us to meet another's needs. Whether you are the receiver or the giver, how you do both should be **different** than what the world does.

LESSON #4: GOD'S PROVISION BRINGS HIM GLORY. PRAISE HIM OPENLY.

Acknowledging that what we have, whether much or little, all comes from God is giving Him glory.

IS GOD DEPENDING ON CHRISTIANS?

True or False? "God is not depending on any government; God is depending on Christians."
FALSE

This statement puts you on a higher level than God so that He becomes dependent on you! Wrong! God does work through Christians to meet the needs of people, but God is not depending on people to do His work. He gives us opportunity and the desire and the provision to share.

REASONS WHY GOD WANTS US TO DEPEND ON HIM MORE THAN ON OURSELVES

- ✓ He initiates the grace of giving. (8:1)
- ✓ We need Him to direct our giving according to His will. (8:5)
- ✓ He makes us spiritually rich so we can give. (8:9)
- ✓ He puts into our hearts concerns for us to have. (8:16)
- ✓ We are His representatives who honor Christ so can be trusted with money handling. (8:23)
- ✓ God blesses us so we can give to others. (9:8)
- ✓ God enlarges the harvest of our generosity and good works. (9:10)
- ✓ God gives through us to meet the needs of His people. (9:12)

Let Jesus satisfy your heart with confidence that you can depend on Him. Then, live each day as a God-dependent woman!

8: Tearing Down Walls

2 Corinthians 10:1-18

The weapons we fight with are not the weapons of the world. On the contrary, they have divine power to demolish strongholds. 5 We demolish arguments and every pretension that sets itself up against the knowledge of God, and we take captive every thought to make it obedient to Christ. (2 Corinthians 10:4-5)

In our study of 2 Corinthians so far, we have seen how the God who comforts us understands the many kinds of suffering we undergo in daily life. Although Paul and his friends experienced a lot of persecution that made them fear for their lives, suffering doesn't only come from persecution. Suffering can be caused by physical danger and financial hardships. It can also come from within your circle of friends, including those whom you love the most. Misunderstandings, behavioral conflicts, and slanderous information from others can cause hurt feelings and mistrust. Regardless of the source, suffering drives us to dependence on God. We set our hope on Him more than on ourselves. We see His love and grace given to us. We trust Him to work in the situation and give thanks. That is dependent living.

In the last lesson, we saw how God teaches His children to be generous to one another as He Himself is a generous giver. This requires that we trust Him with every bit of provision we receive, recognize that it all comes from Him and belongs to Him, then ask Him to guide us as we use what He has provided to us. That is dependent living.

At this point in the letter, Paul begins to hit hard at the charges made against him by his opponents in Corinth. We don't know who they are except that they are Jews (2 Corinthians 11:22). Their teaching may be like the Judaizers that infiltrated the Galatian churches (Jewish Christians insisting Gentiles must be circumcised and follow the Mosaic Law to be saved). We can infer from the text that these false teachers attack those who have influence over the Corinthians (Paul and his companions) in order to gain prestige and power for themselves.

When we are falsely accused, we have a choice. We can choose to get sidetracked by copying the bad behavior of the accusers. Or we can stay on course by continuing to walk faithfully in dependence on God to avenge us and tear down the walls for us. That is also dependent living.

Questions to consider this week:

- Do you recognize a current situation in your life where you're trying to fight a spiritual battle with worldly weapons such as deception, manipulation, and intimidation? How is that working for you?

- Do you have a tendency to compare yourself to others to see how you measure up? Or do you look at the world's standards to define your achievements. How does that affect you?

Day One Study—Get the big picture.

Ask the Lord Jesus to teach you through His Word.

Read the Bible passage below (NIV). Use your own method (colored pencils, lines, shapes) to mark 1) anything that grabs your attention, 2) words you want to understand, and 3) topics you have seen before in this letter. Draw arrows between thoughts that connect. Put a star ✻ next to anything you think relates to dependent living.

10 *By the humility and gentleness of Christ, I appeal to you—I, Paul, who am "timid" when face to face with you, but "bold" toward you when away! 2 I beg you that when I come I may not have to be as bold as I expect to be toward some people who think that we live by the standards of this world. 3 For though we live in the world, we do not wage war as the world does. 4 The weapons we fight with are not the weapons of the world. On the contrary, they have divine power to demolish strongholds. 5 We demolish arguments and every pretension that sets itself up against the knowledge of God, and we take captive every thought to make it obedient to Christ. 6 And we will be ready to punish every act of disobedience, once your obedience is complete.*

7 You are judging by appearances. If anyone is confident that they belong to Christ, they should consider again that we belong to Christ just as much as they do. 8 So even if I boast somewhat freely about the authority the Lord gave us for building you up rather than tearing you down, I will not be ashamed of it. 9 I do not want to seem to be trying to frighten you with my letters. 10 For some say, "His letters are weighty and forceful, but in person he is unimpressive and his speaking amounts to nothing." 11 Such people should realize that what we are in our letters when we are absent, we will be in our actions when we are present.

12 We do not dare to classify or compare ourselves with some who commend themselves. When they measure themselves by themselves and compare themselves with themselves, they are not wise. 13 We, however, will not boast beyond proper limits, but will confine our boasting to the sphere of service God himself has assigned to us, a sphere that also includes you. 14 We are not going too far in our boasting, as would be the case if we had not come to you, for we did get as far as you with the gospel of Christ. 15 Neither do we go beyond our limits by boasting of work done by others. Our hope is that, as your faith continues to grow, our sphere of activity among you will greatly expand, 16 so that we can preach the gospel in the regions beyond you. For we do not want to boast about work already done in someone else's territory. 17 But, "Let the one who boasts boast in the Lord." 18 For it is not the one who commends himself who is approved, but the one whom the Lord commends.

1. What grabbed your attention from these verses?

    - 10:1-6

    - 10:7-11

LESSON EIGHT

- 10:12-18

2. What verses or specific words do you want to understand better?

3. What topics are repeated in this passage or continue an earlier discussion in this letter?

4. What verses illustrate or help you understand what dependent living on God looks like?

Respond to the Lord about what He has shown you today.

Day Two Study

Read 2 Corinthians 10:1-6. Ask the Lord Jesus to teach you through His Word.

> **Scriptural Insight:** Look at v. 1. Whenever Paul described himself as "I Paul," he is making his point with strong emphasis and telling them that what he is about to say is indeed coming from him. See where he does this in Galatians 5:2; Ephesians 3:1; Colossians 1:23; 1 Thessalonians 2:18; 2 Thessalonians 3:17; and Philemon 19.

What does the Bible say?

5. Paul addresses accusations made against him that he is "timid." He responds with truth. By what does Paul make his appeal to the Corinthians (v. 1 first part)?

THE GOD-DEPENDENT WOMAN

How has he been described (v. 1 second part)?

Some people think what about Paul and his team (v. 2)?

Though we live in the world (in the flesh), we do not do what (v. 3)?

Our weapons (v. 4) are not _____

but they have _____.

We are to demolish what (v. 5)?

We are to take captive what (v. 5)?

What will we be ready to do (v. 6)?

Did anything else grab your attention?

> **Historical Insight:** The word picture Paul used in v. 5 is that of Roman siege warfare focused on tearing down walls of a fortified city in order to take it captive.

What does it mean?

6. Review the first part of 2 Corinthians 10:1 then read the "Focus on the Meaning" below.

   > **Focus on the Meaning:** Humility and gentleness were characteristics of Christ. Humility recognizes God as one's authority and takes a servant attitude toward people. Gentleness refers to strength under control and is expressed through fairness and graciousness to others. Both are available to us under the control of Christ who is in us. Both are evidence of dependent living.

   How has Paul's behavior toward the Corinthians been like this? Note: We will address the rest of v. 1 in the Day Three Study.

LESSON EIGHT

Since the fall of humans in the garden (Genesis 3), there has been a spiritual war raging in our world concerning God's truth versus lies being disseminated through human reasoning and demonic influence. One leads to overflowing joy and dependent living on God. The other leads to self-dependence and rebellion against God. Let's look at this warfare more closely.

7. **Truth #1: We have God's power and ways to fight the war effectively**. Note: The context in vv. 3-4 is the Church.

   - What are we fighting against? See also 2 Corinthians 2:11; 4:4; Ephesians 2:1-3; and 1 John 2:16.

   - Fill out the chart below to compare what weapons we should and should not use in this spiritual warfare.

2 Corinthians verses	What we should not use	What we can and should use
1:12		
4:2, 5		
5:16		
6:6-7, 14-16		
7:2		
10:1, 4		

THE GOD-DEPENDENT WOMAN

Think About It: Weapons such as intimidation, manipulation, trickery, double-talk, rumor, and hypocritical behavior are not from the Spirit of God and are not acceptable weapons for the believer to use in spiritual warfare. Victory comes from approaching life (and battles) God's way and relying on His power to overcome the enemy.

8. **Truth #2: We have God's power to demolish strongholds.** Strongholds are anything upon which one relies for security and survival. Think "castle" or "fortress." But these are not good castles. They are anything that takes captive the minds of believers away from depending on God. Paul references arguments and pretensions raised up against the knowledge of God.

    From the Greek: "Arguments" comes from the Greek *logismos*, meaning "thoughts, calculations, and reasonings." Paul uses that to represent walls of wrong thinking standing in opposition to right Christian thinking. "Pretension" comes from the Greek *hypsoma*, meaning "elevated structure such as a barrier or rampart." This represents a notion contrary to God that's been raised up or lifted high with the purpose to intimidate. (Kelly Minter, *All Things New*, p. 141)

    - Give some examples of strongholds that affect believers today.

    - To demolish a physical stronghold takes power and strategy. Using what you have learned from 2 Corinthians, how are Christians to demolish spiritual strongholds?

    Think About It: Satan's strategy uses speculations (theories) and incorrect information that contradict God's revealed truth. When approaching Bible Study, beware of speculating just to derive an answer. That would include reading into Scripture what we want it to say to match what our culture is teaching us. God has revealed much for us to know. Some things He has reserved for Himself (Deut. 29:29).

9. To complete tearing down these walls (v. 5), means you must take captive every thought to make it obedient to Christ (a continuous action). How would you do that for a spiritual stronghold in your life?

10. Strongholds are not just thoughts but can be associated with people who have influence over you. What should you also do? See 2 Corinthians 6:14-7:1 and 1 Corinthians 15:33.

LESSON EIGHT

Focus on the Meaning: Based on 2 Corinthians 10:2 and 6, the Corinthians needed to make a clean break from the rebels in their midst. Paul needed the church to stand firm with him in disciplining his unrepentant opponents and removing themselves from that influence.

11. What else did you learn as you studied 2 Corinthians 10:1-6?

What application will you make after studying today's passage?

12. Do you recognize a current situation in your life where you are trying to fight a spiritual battle with worldly weapons such as deception, manipulation, and intimidation? How is that working for you?

- Follow the steps below to recognize and demolish any strongholds in your reasoning and thoughts that work against the knowledge of God and dependency on Him.
    - ✓ Ask God to help you identify the toxic thought patterns you have been building in your mind that work against the knowledge of God and your dependency on Him.
    - ✓ Give those to God and ask Him to help you knock them down with truth.
    - ✓ Trust God to help you destroy the stronghold by consistently applying the truth.

> To get help recognizing cultural strongholds that affect you or your children, check out the podcasts on mamabearapologetics.com.

13. In what other ways can you apply this lesson to your life?

Respond to the Lord about what He has shown you today.

THE GOD-DEPENDENT WOMAN

Day Three Study

Read 2 Corinthians 10:7-11. Ask the Lord Jesus to teach you through His Word.

The word "boast" occurs twenty-nine times in this letter, and only twenty-six times in all the other letters put together. Paul used this conflict with the Corinthians as a "teachable moment" for them on what validates boasting for a believer. His words are still extremely relevant for us today as we learn to live dependently on the Lord.

What does the Bible say?

14. Let's continue to explore the gracious yet unbending ways in which Paul addressed his opponents.

    Though Bible translations of the beginning of v. 7 differ, we can conclude from the context of vv. 1 and 10 that Paul is telling them to look at the facts and not just outward appearances.

    What does Paul say to the one confident in belonging to Christ (the rest of v. 7)?

    About what does he boast freely (v. 8)?

    What are the troublemakers saying about Paul (vv. 9-10)? See also v. 1.

    What does Paul say in response (v. 11)?

    Did anything else grab your attention?

    > **Scriptural Insight:** Like so many who judge things according to the outward display of this world, Paul's opponents interpreted meekness (humility) as weakness, forbearance as cowardice, and gentleness as indecision (cf. v. 1; 11:21)—or at least they had sought to induce the Corinthians to place this interpretation on Paul's character. (*Dr. Constable's Notes on 2 Corinthians 2017 Edition*, p. 101)

What does it mean?

15. Regarding verse 7, Paul briefly mentioned this in 2 Corinthians 5:12, 16. He is getting back to it now. What is he reminding them to do? Why is that important? See also your answers to Q10.

LESSON EIGHT

16. Paul refers to his authority in v. 8. Referring back to v. 1, Paul said he was letting Christ's humility and gentleness live through him as he exhorted the Corinthians in a gracious manner. He also states that spiritual authority is to be used for building up other believers and not tearing them down. How are the false teachers who claim to be Christians not adhering to this principle regarding Paul and his team? Hint: what are they saying about their Christian brother Paul?

Focus on the Meaning: This does not mean Paul—or any spiritual leaders for that matter—should be a pushover who never enforces any rules. Here's where the good tension of extending grace and applying discipline comes into play. We need the discernment of the Holy Spirit to know when to emphasize each. (Kelly Minter, *All Things New, p. 148)*

17. Though Paul might not be the flashy speaker like the professional orators of his day, from where did the power and influence of his teaching come so people should follow him? See 1 Corinthians 1:17; 2:1-5 and 2 Corinthians 11:6,10.

Think About It: In 1 Corinthians 11:1, Paul says, "Follow my example, as I follow the example of Christ." That's the kind of statement that gets the apostle Paul slapped with labels like "arrogant" and "egotistical." Maybe that bothers you, too. Why didn't Paul just take himself out of the equation and tell people to follow Christ? The answer is that Paul knew we all need a role model, a picture of Christ that makes the heart, mind and ways of Christ visible and tangible. To step into a role of leadership is essentially to state, "Follow me as I follow Christ." If people are going to follow us, our primary task is following well ... We all follow somebody. If you are a Christ follower, the practice of following well may be one of the greatest tests of your character. Who are you following? (Heather Zempel, *Community Is Messy*, pages 67-68)

18. What else did you learn as you studied 2 Corinthians 10:7-11?

THE GOD-DEPENDENT WOMAN

What application will you make?

19. All of us have spheres of authority. We are to use our authority for building up those in our sphere of influence. Some of us don't handle that authority well.

    - Do you struggle with being bossy and bearing down on others within your sphere of influence? What is the evidence and fruit of your behavior? Ask the Lord to teach you graciousness and gentleness.

    - Are you continually being walked over and struggle to assert your God-given authority in an area of your life? What is the evidence and fruit of your behavior? Ask the Lord to help you step up and lead with courage for the sake of building others up.

    - For both you can say, "Lord Jesus, I can't do this on my own. But you can do this in me and through me. I will trust you to show me how."

20. We should be careful how we talk about other Christian teachers / leaders. Review 2 Corinthians 10:7-8. We are to demolish arguments, not people. What if you have a disagreement with other believers, perhaps a former church you attended or the leaders of a ministry? Usually it is over leadership style or preferences.

    - As you talk to the Lord about the situation, what questions should you ask yourself?

    - If the Lord leads you to approach the ones in charge of that ministry, what questions should you ask them?

    - What should you avoid doing so as not to "wage a worldly war" against brothers and sisters in Christ? Review the "Think About It" after Question 7.

21. In what other ways can you apply this lesson to your life?

Respond to the Lord about what He has shown you today.

LESSON EIGHT

DAY FOUR STUDY

Read 2 Corinthians 10:12-18. Ask the Lord Jesus to teach you through His Word.

What does the Bible say?

> **Historical Insight:** The Greek philosopher Aristides said that on every street in Corinth one met a so-called wise man, who had his own solutions to the world's problems. (*NIV Study Bible,* note on 1 Corinthians 1:19, p. 1736) Does this sound familiar to today's world?

22. Paul helps the Corinthians to recognize what true wisdom is and what is really worth boasting about.

    What does Paul not do (v. 12)?

    What does he say is unwise?

    To what does Paul confine his boasting (vv. 13-14)?

    What is Paul's hope (vv. 15-16 first part)?

    What does he not want to do (v. 16 second part)?

    In whom should we boast (v. 17)? See also 1 Corinthians 1:31.

    For it is not the one who _____ who is approved, but the one whom _____ (v. 18).

    Did anything else grab your attention?

> **Focus on the Meaning:** Paul did "pioneer evangelism." He did not want to build on, much less take credit for, the foundation work that anyone else had done, but to "preach the gospel" in previously unevangelized areas. He did not, however, object to others building on the foundation that he had laid, or watering what he had planted (1 Corinthians 3:6, 10). He did object to their failing to give credit where credit was due. (*Dr. Constable's Notes on 2 Corinthians 2017 Edition*, p. 103)

THE GOD-DEPENDENT WOMAN

What does it mean?

23. Looking specifically at verse 12. Read this verse in the NLT for additional understanding. Comparison is a huge issue for some people. Paul says it is not wise to compare yourself with those who commend themselves and even measure themselves by themselves.

    - Why is that not wise?

    - What would that kind of comparison look like? Give examples from your culture.

    Think About It: Comparison against a standard isn't all bad. But comparison becomes dangerous when that standard is based on worldly values, and we deem ourselves "successful" when we hit that worldly standard. With the prevalence of social media, we can be tempted to compare ourselves with other believers—their achievements, social platform, and even their recreational activities. This can lead to self-centered pride or feelings of discouragement and failure. Also, don't glorify men or women by 1) depending on them more than on Christ, 2) crediting them for your spiritual blessings, or 3) namedropping to increase your own image. Gratitude is okay. ☺

24. ✱ The answer to this "comparison thinking" is in vv. 17-18. Considering what you have learned so far in 2 Corinthians, why should we boast about the Lord and not about ourselves? See also John 5:44 and Jeremiah 29:23-24 (the Old Testament source for Paul's quote).

    Focus on the Meaning: The word Paul kept using for "boast" means "to glory in or on something, to rejoice." Boasting is not bad if you are boasting about the Lord and His work (v. 17) and the assignment He has given you (v. 13).

25. What else did you learn as you studied 2 Corinthians 10:12-18?

LESSON EIGHT

What application will you make?

26. Do you have a tendency to compare yourself to others to see how you measure up? Or do you look at the world's standards to define your achievements? How does that affect you?

27. ✸ Consider vv. 13-14. How does living dependently on Christ keep you focused on what He has appointed YOU to be and do?

28. In what other ways can you apply this lesson to your life?

29. Review the passage for this lesson in "Day One Study." Add reasons why God wants us to depend on Him more than on ourselves to the chart below. I have given a few prompts.

Verse(s)	Reasons why God wants us to depend on Him more than on ourselves
10:1	So we can treat others with the humility and gentleness of Christ
10:3-4	We need His power to demolish strongholds holding us captive
10:5	We need His power to take captive our thoughts for Him
10:13	To find our sphere of service He has assigned to us

129

Respond to the Lord about what He has shown you today.

As His child, God transforms your life by teaching you to live dependently on Him in weakness and in strength.

> **Recommended:** Listen to "Grasping Truth Protects You from Enemy Captivity" to reinforce what you have learned. Use the following listener guide.

LESSON EIGHT

PODCAST LISTENER GUIDE

Grasping Truth Protects You from Enemy Captivity

RECOGNIZING SOMEONE WHO IS TAKEN CAPTIVE AWAY FROM CHRIST

- Influential fakers know how to get women to follow them. *2 Timothy 3:6-7*

- Women who never recognize and grasp biblical truth will be taken captive by whatever flashy teachings that come along and live unsatisfied, unstable lives. *Ephesians 4:14*

GRASPING TRUTH PROTECTS FROM ENEMY CAPTIVITY

- To protect yourself from enemy captivity, renew your mind through knowing the Bible, which is God's truth and through letting the Holy Spirit implant that truth in your mind so you can understand it. Then, you can diffuse arguments against the knowledge of God that are influencing you, and you can take captive your thoughts, making them obedient to Christ.

- The writings of the New Testament are historically reliable and, therefore, can be trusted.

DWELL IN TRUTH YOU CAN KNOW.

- To dwell in truth is to make your home there. That means God's truth dominates your thoughts and attitudes, governs your life, and satisfies your heart.

- God gives us plenty of truth in the Bible that we can know and trust. 66 books, 1189 chapters!

- God wants us to know the truth He has revealed to us, to make our home in that truth. *Ephesians 1:17-19*

HUMBLY ACCEPT WHAT YOU DON'T KNOW OR UNDERSTAND.

- Some things we read in the Bible we don't understand now but might in the future. There is much we can know now. But there are things we will never know or understand. *Deuteronomy 29:29*

- We'll never know all there is to know about God. There will always be some mystery about Him. But there is enough revealed in the Bible to satisfy your desire to **know Him truthfully** and to know how to live your life in Christ truthfully.

DISCERN ALL TEACHING THROUGH THE COMPLETE REVELATION OF GOD'S WORD.

1. Evaluate what you read and hear by comparing it with the whole Bible.

- Read any verse in the context of the passage where it is found—the paragraph, the chapter, and the book.

THE GOD-DEPENDENT WOMAN

- Examine the original words to see what the writer meant and what the audience likely understood.

- Look at other verses with similar content to let the Bible interpret itself. And you should always ask the Holy Spirit for understanding.

2. Avoid the "look-imagine-see dragon" when viewing any verse.

The "look-imagine-see dragon" shows up this way: someone *looks* at a verse or passage, *imagines* what they want it to say, then in their mind *sees* what they have imagined through twisting word meanings and interpretations. Once it starts, it's like a fiery dragon burning truth in its path. Cultural influence on Bible study feeds this dragon.

- Tame the "look-imagine-see dragon" by considering the Bible as sufficient on its own, not needing our "improvement."

- Tame the "look-imagine-see dragon" by basing your faith on what **is** in God's Word, not something you have just heard about it and not something you're imagining to be there.

- Tame the "look-imagine-see dragon" by following the inductive process for Bible Study—observation, interpretation, and application. Then, you can dwell in truth you can know.

DOES GOD HELP THOSE WHO HELP THEMSELVES?

> ***True or False?*** *"God helps those who help themselves. Our safety and survival in life do not depend on direct divine intervention, but on our ability to see and willingness to seize opportunities to save ourselves."* **FALSE**

This is very humanistic, saying basically you can do this if you are smart enough to seize opportunities to save yourself. As we have studied in 2 Corinthians, the Bible teaches that we are to depend on God and let Him show us how to respond to a situation.

REASONS WHY GOD WANTS US TO DEPEND ON HIM MORE THAN ON OURSELVES

- ✓ So we can treat others with the humility and gentleness of Christ. (10:1)
- ✓ We need His power to demolish strongholds holding us captive. (10:3-4)
- ✓ We need His power to take captive our thoughts for Him. (10:5)
- ✓ So we use our authority to build others up and not tear them down. (10:8)
- ✓ To find our sphere of service He has assigned to us. (10:13)
- ✓ To confine our boasting to the Lord and the sphere of service He has assigned to us. (10:13)
- ✓ So we will seek our approval and commendation from Him rather than others. (10:17)

Let Jesus satisfy your heart with confidence that you can depend on Him. Then, live each day as a God-dependent woman!

9: Live to Serve Christ through Anything

2 Corinthians 11:1-33

If I must boast, I will boast of the things that show my weakness. The God and Father of the Lord Jesus, who is to be praised forever, knows that I am not lying. (2 Corinthians 11:30-31)

Why is Paul even bothering to write this letter? He loves the Corinthian believers. He spent more than a year and a half of his life there giving birth to the church. He made friends. He poured into them. He loved them. Yet, the relationship has been very rocky.

Even in the mess of this rocky relationship with people he dearly loves, and whom Christ dearly loves, Paul writes to them in 1 Corinthians 11:1, "Follow my example, as I follow the example of Christ." Paul desired to be for them an exemplary role mode, a picture of Christ that makes the heart, mind, and ways of Christ visible and tangible. He lives out his life as a servant of God in every way—in good times and in very hard times.

While those influencing his Corinthian family are claiming to be "super-apostles," they are actually deceivers, masquerading as servants of light but really being used as servants of Satan instead. Paul emerges as the truly Spirit-led apostle. He is the one following Christ.

If people are going to follow us, our primary task is to test whom we are following. We all follow somebody. If you are a Christ follower, the practice of following Him well may be one of the greatest tests of your character. Whom are you following?

Questions to consider this week:

- How do you give your preparations and skills to God and desire that the power of God will shine His light through you—at work, at home, in the neighborhood, in the school, and elsewhere?

- How do you recognize if someone exercising spiritual authority over you is a true servant of the Lord Jesus and not someone masquerading as a servant of righteousness?

- When it comes to the troubles and difficulties of life, how can we more consciously focus on what Jesus can do or has done for us rather than focusing on what He has not done?

Day One Study—Get the big picture.

Ask the Lord Jesus to teach you through His Word.

Read the Bible passage below (NIV, including verses from the last lesson). Use your own method (colored pencils, lines, shapes) to mark 1) anything that grabs your attention, 2) words you want to understand, and 3) topics you have seen before in this letter. Draw arrows between thoughts that connect. Put a star ✱ next to anything you think relates to dependent living.

10 *12 We do not dare to classify or compare ourselves with some who commend themselves. When they measure themselves by themselves and compare themselves with themselves, they are not wise. 13 We, however, will not boast beyond proper limits, but will confine our boasting to the sphere of service God himself has assigned to us, a sphere that also includes you. 14 We are not going too far in our boasting, as would be the case if we had not come to you, for we did get as far as you with the gospel of Christ. 15 Neither do we go beyond our limits by boasting of work done by others. Our hope is that, as your faith continues to grow, our sphere of activity among you will greatly expand, 16 so that we can preach the gospel in the regions beyond you. For we do not want to boast about work already done in someone else's territory. 17 But, "Let the one who boasts boast in the Lord." 18 For it is not the one who commends himself who is approved, but the one whom the Lord commends.*

11 *I hope you will put up with me in a little foolishness. Yes, please put up with me! 2 I am jealous for you with a godly jealousy. I promised you to one husband, to Christ, so that I might present you as a pure virgin to him. 3 But I am afraid that just as Eve was deceived by the serpent's cunning, your minds may somehow be led astray from your sincere and pure devotion to Christ. 4 For if someone comes to you and preaches a Jesus other than the Jesus we preached, or if you receive a different spirit from the Spirit you received, or a different gospel from the one you accepted, you put up with it easily enough.*

5 I do not think I am in the least inferior to those "super-apostles." 6 I may indeed be untrained as a speaker, but I do have knowledge. We have made this perfectly clear to you in every way.

7 Was it a sin for me to lower myself in order to elevate you by preaching the gospel of God to you free of charge? 8 I robbed other churches by receiving support from them so as to serve you. 9 And when I was with you and needed something, I was not a burden to anyone, for the brothers who came from Macedonia supplied what I needed. I have kept myself from being a burden to you in any way, and will continue to do so. 10 As surely as the truth of Christ is in me, nobody in the regions of Achaia will stop this boasting of mine. 11 Why? Because I do not love you? God knows I do!

12 And I will keep on doing what I am doing in order to cut the ground from under those who want an opportunity to be considered equal with us in the things they boast about. 13 For such people are false apostles, deceitful workers, masquerading as apostles of Christ. 14 And no wonder, for Satan himself masquerades as an angel of light. 15 It is not surprising, then, if his servants also masquerade as servants of righteousness. Their end will be what their actions deserve.

16 I repeat: Let no one take me for a fool. But if you do, then tolerate me just as you would a fool, so that I may do a little boasting. 17 In this self-confident boasting I am not talking as the Lord would, but as a fool. 18 Since many are boasting in the way the world does, I too will boast. 19 You gladly put up with fools since you are so wise! 20 In fact, you even put up with anyone who enslaves you or exploits you or takes advantage of you or puts on airs or slaps you in the face. 21 To my shame I admit that we were too weak for that!

LESSON NINE

Whatever anyone else dares to boast about—I am speaking as a fool—I also dare to boast about. 22 Are they Hebrews? So am I. Are they Israelites? So am I. Are they Abraham's descendants? So am I. 23 Are they servants of Christ? (I am out of my mind to talk like this.) I am more. I have worked much harder, been in prison more frequently, been flogged more severely, and been exposed to death again and again. 24 Five times I received from the Jews the forty lashes minus one. 25 Three times I was beaten with rods, once I was pelted with stones, three times I was shipwrecked, I spent a night and a day in the open sea, 26 I have been constantly on the move. I have been in danger from rivers, in danger from bandits, in danger from my fellow Jews, in danger from Gentiles; in danger in the city, in danger in the country, in danger at sea; and in danger from false believers. 27 I have labored and toiled and have often gone without sleep; I have known hunger and thirst and have often gone without food; I have been cold and naked. 28 Besides everything else, I face daily the pressure of my concern for all the churches. 29 Who is weak, and I do not feel weak? Who is led into sin, and I do not inwardly burn?

30 If I must boast, I will boast of the things that show my weakness. 31 The God and Father of the Lord Jesus, who is to be praised forever, knows that I am not lying. 32 In Damascus the governor under King Aretas had the city of the Damascenes guarded in order to arrest me. 33 But I was lowered in a basket from a window in the wall and slipped through his hands.

1. What grabbed your attention from these verses?

    - 11:1-15

    - 11:16-21

    - 11:22-33

2. What verses or specific words do you want to understand better?

3. What topics are repeated in this passage or continue an earlier discussion in this letter?

THE GOD-DEPENDENT WOMAN

4. What verses illustrate or help you understand what dependent living on God looks like?

Respond to the Lord about what He has shown you today.

DAY TWO STUDY

Read 2 Corinthians 11:1-15. Ask the Lord Jesus to teach you through His Word.

What does the Bible say?

5. Answer the questions below based on what is in the biblical text. Paul asks them to put up with him and then gives reasons why. Paul asks them to put up with him and gives reasons why.

    What is the reason for Paul's godly jealousy (v. 2)?

    What is his fear (v. 3)?

    What 3 distortions of teaching did Paul point out (v. 4)?

    What is their response to the teaching that might be leading them astray (end of v. 4)?

    What 3 things does Paul say about himself (vv. 5-6)?

    What did Paul do while in Corinth that was opposite of expectations (v. 7)?

    Who took care of his financial needs (vv. 8-9)? See also Acts 18:3-5.

    What will he continue to do (v. 9)?

LESSON NINE

What does he declare about his feelings for the Corinthians (v. 11)?

Why will Paul keep on doing what he is doing (v. 12)?

How does Paul describe the slanderers (v. 13)?

Who do these pretenders actually represent (vv. 14-15)?

Did anything else grab your attention?

> **Focus on the Meaning:** Not all fear is bad. Fear is a normal human emotion designed by God to alert you to danger so you will take action against it. That is what Paul is doing regarding his beloved Christian brothers and sisters.

What does it mean?

Paul's jealousy was in line with God's purposes. The false teachers were not only calling his apostolic authority into question. They were also leading the Corinthians astray from pure devotion to Christ. This was serious.

6. Contrast jealousy "of someone" with jealousy "for someone."

> **Focus on the Meaning:** There is a place for a spiritual father's / mother's passionate concern for the exclusive and pure devotion to Christ of their spiritual children, and also a place for anger at potential violators of that purity (11:29). (*Dr. Constable's Notes on 2 Corinthians 2017 Edition*, p. 105)
>
> **Think About It:** Leaders who can't be questioned end up doing questionable things. (Jon Acuff)

7. Though not a trained speaker, Paul said he had knowledge (v. 6).

   - What kind of knowledge does Paul have?

   - Why is this more important than presentation? See 2 Corinthians 4:6-7 and 1 Corinthians 2:1-5.

Think About It: Paul didn't pretend to be one of those dazzlers the Greeks valued. But the listeners were stirred by his words and grew in their knowledge of and relationship with God because of his teaching. The world has plenty of dazzlers. Lost and confused people need to meet someone with abiding spiritual wisdom and knowledge about what truly matters. It is okay to have godly dazzlers pointing us to dependence on God as Paul did. That is what matters.

8. One of the accusations against Paul centered around how he differed from the usual professional speakers who expected the listeners to pay for their "wisdom." Such money given also gave the audience a measure of control over the speaker (permission) and the speaker control over the audience (influence). Keep in mind that Greek culture considered manual labor such as Paul's tent making to be "lower class."

   - Was it wrong for Paul to preach the gospel free of charge?

   - What reason did Paul give for choosing to humbly serve the Corinthians like that?

   - How is what he did an application of Jesus' words in Mark 10:38-45?

   Scriptural Insight: Paul's principle was to preach and teach without charging those who benefited directly from his ministry. This is a good policy in church planting, but it is not normative for a settled pastoral ministry (1 Corinthians 9:14; 1 Timothy 5:17-18). (*Dr. Constable's Notes on 2 Corinthians 2017 Edition,* p. 108)

9. Recognizing false teachers:
   - Paul brought up 3 distortions of teaching in v. 4 that had happened or was happening to the Corinthians. Read Galatians 1:6-9 where he mentioned something similar. How do you recognize whether someone is teaching a different Jesus, spirit, or gospel?

   - Looking at vv. 13-15 and 23. Paul said the false teachers were masquerading as servants of righteousness. How does this description add to the seriousness of his warning?

LESSON NINE

Scriptural Insight: The false teachers may have been genuine believers. Or at least they called themselves Christians (verse 23). Yet, they were following the example of Satan more than Christ. They perverted the thinking of the Corinthians which led their affections away from Paul and Christ as well (verse 3).

10. What else did you learn as you studied 2 Corinthians 11:1-15?

What application will you make?

Paul was a successful church planter, a gifted teacher, and excellent writer. Yet, he gave all those strengths to the Lord and still depended on the Lord as he accomplished those tasks.

11. It is okay to prepare and refine your skills and talents, especially as you want them to be used for God's purposes. What would it look like for you to give your preparations to God and desire that the power of God will shine His light through you? A good question to ask yourself regarding your strengths is this, "Am I living in self-sufficiency or God-dependency?"

    - At work

    - At home

    - In the church

12. Doing everything right does not always stop people from trying to slander and discredit you. How does Paul's example help you deal with false information about you?

13. In what other ways can you apply this lesson to your life?

Respond to the Lord about what He has shown you today.

Day Three Study

Read 2 Corinthians 11:16-21 first part. Ask the Lord Jesus to teach you through His Word.

What does the Bible say?

> **From the Greek:** A "fool" in Hellenistic-Roman society was one who had lost the correct measure of himself and the world around them.

14. The Corinthians have been putting up with the teaching of fools, contrary to the solid, biblical truth that Paul taught them. The foolish teachers claimed to be God's leaders but were more interested in their own position and power. Paul had no choice but to refute them for the sake of the church he loved. He creatively uses sarcasm to make the Corinthians recognize what was happening. He answered the fools "according to their folly" Proverbs 26:5)

    What does Paul ask of them in v. 16?

    Many are boasting how (v. 18)?

    What does he say they are gladly doing (v. 19)?

    He says they put up with anyone who does what 5 things to them (v. 20)?

    What did Paul not do to the Corinthians (v. 21 first half of verse)?

    Did anything else grab your attention?

What does it mean?

Remember that the false teachers were masquerading as apostles of Christ and servants of righteousness. Judging by physical appearances, they most likely didn't look like evil people (vv. 13-15). Their teaching and behavior betrayed their motives.

15. Bad teaching and dictatorial behavior (vv. 3-4, 19-20) lead to exploitation—what we might even call cultic behavior, including the kind of treatment listed. Who is vulnerable to that kind of exploitation? Why?

LESSON NINE

Think About It: According to 1 Corinthians 8:1, knowledge puffs up (makes proud, inflates ego). Depending on one's own "wisdom" can lead to foolish choices and susceptibility to being ensnared by false teaching. The answer is to know Christ, embrace God's grace and the truth of His Word, and live confidently in your identity. Then you can say "no" to such foolishness from bad teaching.

16. How was Paul's approach to ministry with the Corinthians different from that of the false teachers? What Christ-like characteristics did Paul display? Use what you have learned so far in 2 Corinthians to get your answer.

17. What else did you learn as you studied 2 Corinthians 11:16-21?

What application will you make?

From the Greek: Back in 2 Corinthians 4:2, Paul said that he did not use deception or distort the Word of God like those who masqueraded as servants of righteousness were doing. The Greek word from which we get "distort" primarily signifies "to ensnare," especially by mingling the truth of the Word of God with false doctrines or notions, and so handling it "deceitfully." (Kelly Minter, *All Things New*, p. 55)

Distortion of God's Word plays out in many ways. It is especially done to justify some behavior that the false teachers want to engage in themselves. Or it can happen when a spiritual leader uses a verse to shame, manipulate, or condemn you for something already forgiven by Christ.

18. You may be wondering how you can tell if someone exercising authority over you is a true servant of the Lord Jesus and not someone masquerading as a servant of righteousness and exploiting you.

    - Based upon what you have learned in 2 Corinthians 11:1-21, what questions should you ask to determine if this is happening to you?

    - What should / can you do to get freed from this exploitation?

141

19. Have you fallen victim to a "distortion of the Word of God" in the past? What was taught, and how did you get freed from that?

Scriptural Insight: A common false teaching says that women are more easily deceived than men because of what happened in Genesis 3. That is NOT a biblical truth. Dr. Sandra Glahn, gender studies professor at Dallas Theological Seminary, explains it this way, "What is significant about the man and woman in [Genesis 3] is that they both rebelled. ... Being seduced by evil is a human thing, not a woman thing—as Paul mentions when warning the Corinthians (2 Corinthians 11:3). The Bible does not teach that because Eve was deceived, all women are more easily deceived than men. Nor does the Scripture teach that all women excel at seducing and deceiving (these ideas are contradictions, anyway—one cannot be a master of deception while also being easily duped)." (Sandra Glahn, *"Biblical Womanhood": What is a Woman?* accessed online at Bible.org)

20. In what other ways can you apply this lesson to your life?

Respond to the Lord about what He has shown you today.

LESSON NINE

DAY FOUR STUDY

Read 2 Corinthians 11:21-33. Ask the Lord Jesus to teach you through His Word.

Paul's approach to ministry was to promote Christ, not himself. Because of the false apostles claiming to be servants of Christ yet denying Paul's authority, Paul felt pressed to talk about his own life choices and experiences, especially hardships. These are evidences of the Lord Jesus' commendation of his work and vindication of him as an apostle (2 Corinthians 10:18). As you study this passage, recognize that many of these challenges can happen to anyone, not just those being persecuted for their faith.

What does the Bible say?

21. Complete the following statements based on what you see in the biblical text. Put a star ✱ next to challenges that any servant of Christ may face in life, including what you might have already experienced.

    What do you learn about the false apostles (vv. 22-23)?

    As a servant of Christ, Paul says he has done what (v. 23)?

    As a servant of Christ, Paul experienced these things ...

What happened?	How many times?
v. 24	
v. 25	
v. 25	
v. 25	
v. 25	

    As a servant of Christ, he has been constantly on the move (v. 26) and in danger from/in what?

    As a servant of Christ, he has also (v. 27) _____ and gone without _____; he has known _____ and gone without _____; he has been _____.

THE GOD-DEPENDENT WOMAN

As a servant of Christ, what pressure does he face daily (vv. 28-29)?

As a servant of Christ, he chooses to boast of what (v. 30)?

As a servant of Christ, what does he declare (v. 31)?

As a servant of Christ, what happened to him (vv. 32-33)?

Did anything else grab your attention?

> **Historical Insight:** Because Paul's writing of 2 Corinthians fits into Luke's chronology of his life at Acts 20:2, everything that Paul described here occurred before Acts 20:2 and, therefore, before the end of his third missionary journey, arrest, and transport to Rome. Many of these experiences are not even mentioned in Acts.

What does it mean?

22. **Deeper Discoveries (optional):** Read 1 Corinthians 4:1, 9-13. Paul says that God puts his apostles through what to test their faithfulness?

23. As a servant of Christ,
    - What has Paul risked while serving Christ to the Corinthians and to others?

    - How does Paul's example fly in the face of those who teach that health, wealth, protection, and happiness are the expectations for faithful Christians?

    - Was Paul a fool to serve Christ so relentlessly? Why or why not?

LESSON NINE

24. Review 2 Corinthians 11:12, 18, and 21. Paul said that since many were boasting according to the flesh, he would do that, too.

    - What is boasting according to the flesh?

    - Considering Paul's accomplishments, what kind of boasting would you expect him to include in the verses following 11:22?

    - About what does he boast instead in vv. 23-31?

    - Why do you think Paul chose to boast about his weaknesses instead of his strength?

    Think About It: Instead of citing successes that he had experienced in his ministry and any accolades he had received from others, Paul listed what some would consider defeats and speaks of these as victories! They were victories because he depended on God, and God had supernaturally sustained His servant through every hardship he experienced. What he listed was, therefore, the greatest possible proof and vindication that Paul was a genuine apostle. See Question 22.

    Dependent Living: According to 11:33, Paul was dependent on God to rescue him. God used people to do His work. Paul could do nothing on his own except get in the basket, be quiet, and trust the rope holders. See Acts 9:24-25. God helps those who trust in Him. He uses people as His helpers. You might be that basket provider or the rope holder for someone.

25. What else did you learn as you studied 2 Corinthians 11:21-33?

    Think About It: The Christian life is impossible to live without 2 Corinthians. This letter calms us into settled assurance that it is in the adversities of life in this fallen world, not by avoiding adversity, that life with God blossoms. Ease of life results in frothiness of life. The most substantial, radiant men and women we meet are those who bear scars, who have endured dark valleys. ... we all walk through pain. In different ways, for different reasons, at different seasons of life, hardship washes over

THE GOD-DEPENDENT WOMAN

us. How could we possibly remain sane and cheerful without God's insistence throughout this letter that his deepest consolations are mediated to us in, not after, sorrow? ... The way to joy is actually Christ Himself, walking with Him day by day. And the enjoyment of this Friend tends to rise as circumstances around us fall. (Dane C. Ortlund, *Why Study the Book of 2 Corinthians?* posted online August 2, 2016)

What application will you make?

26. When it comes to the troubles and difficulties of life, how can we more consciously focus on what Jesus can do or has done for us rather than focusing on what He hasn't done?

27. Paul faced daily pressures of responsibility. What pressures come upon you daily? What is your usual response to them? Based on what you have learned from Paul's example, how can you handle daily pressures as a servant of Christ should?

28. In what other ways can you apply this lesson to your life?

29. Review the passage for this lesson in "Day One Study." Add reasons why God wants us to depend on Him more than on ourselves to the chart below. I have given a few prompts.

Verse(s)	Reasons why God wants us to depend on Him more than on ourselves
11:3	To keep us from being led astray by false teaching
11:4-5	To help us recognize error in teaching
11:6	To know the truth about God
11:7-9	For financial support that enables us to share Christ and disciple others

LESSON NINE

Respond to the Lord about what He has shown you today.

As His child, God transforms your life by teaching you to live dependently on Him in weakness and in strength.

> **Recommended:** Listen to "Response to Hardships Reveals Whom We Are Following" to reinforce what you have learned. Use the following listener guide.

Response to Hardships Reveals Whom We Are Following

RECOGNIZING THE DECEIVERS

- Deceivers masquerade as servants of light but are really being used as servants of Satan instead. Christian or not Christians, they are doing Satan's work.

- The mark of a trustworthy teacher is following Christ more than their own preferences and more than the culture. The listeners grow in their knowledge of and relationship with God because of the teaching.

- We can recognize someone masquerading as a servant of light by the fruit of their work.

- We all follow somebody. If you are a Christ follower, the practice of following Him well may be one of the greatest tests of your character.

RESPONSE TO HARDSHIPS, SUFFERING, AND PRESSURE

- Paul boasted about things that others would consider defeats instead. He boasted about how much he depended on the Lord, magnifying the amazing grace of God which is sufficient for his every need. Jesus never failed him. Yet, Jesus allowed him to experience all that pain and suffering.

- What is absolutely amazing is the number of times the Bible says that Paul is joyful and rejoicing during those extremes.

EXPECTATIONS OF ACCEPTABLE OUTCOMES CAN BECOME SINKHOLES FOR US

- Two types of storms hit us—those caused by our own disobedience and those that hit through no fault of our own.

- When we go through such difficulties of life, we all have what we would consider acceptable outcomes. But those expectations can become sinkholes if we try to hold onto them too tightly.

JOY REQUIRES US TO RELEASE OUR EXPECTATION OF ACCEPTABLE OUTCOMES

- When we approach troubles with expectations of what we think are acceptable outcomes and then something else happens, our disappointment and anger can explode like geysers shooting out of a "now-empty pond."

- We need to hold onto those expected answers with open fingers. We must release them to Jesus, and let Him decide what to do.

LESSON NINE

- Paul gave us an example of how to do that regarding his own life and ministry. *2 Corinthians 5; 11*

    [Paul] could maintain a truly joyful attitude, even in unpleasant circumstances, because he derived his joy from seeing God glorified—rather than from seeing himself exalted. (*Dr. Constable's Notes on Philippians 2019 Edition*)

- He could rejoice at any one of God's acceptable outcomes. You and I can choose to do that, too.

REJOICE AT GOD'S ACCEPTABLE OUTCOME

- When you release your expectation of acceptable outcomes, you can rejoice at what God has done or is going to do instead of complaining about what God did not do.

- We can avoid the sinkholes of unreleased expectations by releasing them. Trust in His goodness in whatever He chooses to do in that situation.

- It is okay to ask for your heart's desire. But leave the decision in His hand. Accept the outcome that He provides. And let Him fill your heart with joy in whatever He chooses to do. Your response to hardship, suffering, and pressure reveals whom you are following—yourself, the world, the devil, or Christ.

DO WE DEPEND ON GOD WHEN EVERYTHING ELSE YOU TRY TO DO FOR YOURSELF FAILS?

True or False? "*Reasons why I depend on God: 1. Because everything else I tried to do for myself failed. The end.*" **FALSE**

Not everything you try to do for yourself will fail. You may be very gifted at doing a lot of things. Depending on God will assure that you will do them His way which will make you more successful at doing anything good than you could do on your own.

REASONS WHY GOD WANTS US TO DEPEND ON HIM MORE THAN ON OURSELVES

- ✓ To keep us from being led astray by false teaching. (11:3)
- ✓ To help us recognize error in teaching. (11:4-5)
- ✓ To know the truth about God. (11:6)
- ✓ For financial support that enables us to share Christ and disciple others. (11:7-9)
- ✓ To show us those masquerading as His servants and release us from their grip. (11:13-15)
- ✓ To rescue us from danger. (11:23-27; 32-33)
- ✓ To help us handle the daily pressures of that which concerns us. (11:28)
- ✓ To teach us the value of boasting about the things that show our weakness and need for Him. (11:30)
- ✓ To keep praising God in all our afflictions. (11:31)

Let Jesus satisfy your heart with confidence that you can depend on Him. Then, live each day as a God-dependent woman!

10: Dependent Living Is Powerful

2 Corinthians 12:1-21

But he said to me, "My grace is sufficient for you, for my power is made perfect in weakness." Therefore I will boast all the more gladly about my weaknesses, so that Christ's power may rest on me. 10 That is why, for Christ's sake, I delight in weaknesses, in insults, in hardships, in persecutions, in difficulties. For when I am weak, then I am strong. (2 Corinthians 12:9-10, Memory Verse #3)

The Corinthians had been putting up with the teaching of fools, contrary to the solid, biblical truth that Paul taught them. The foolish teachers claimed to be God's leaders but were really masquerading as apostles of Christ and servants of righteousness. They didn't look evil, but their teaching and behavior exploited the Christians in Corinth—drawing them away from following Christ more than themselves.

On the other hand, Paul chose to promote Christ, not himself. To counter the evil influence on those whom he loved so dearly, Paul is forced to talk about his own life choices and experiences, especially hardships. These are evidences of the Lord Jesus' commendation of his work and vindication of him as an apostle (2 Corinthians 10:18).

Many of those same challenges can happen to anyone, not just those being persecuted for their faith. In the midst of those messy and often painful circumstances, we also have a choice of whom to promote—ourselves or Christ. On whom will we rely at those times? It is in our weaknesses that He is the strongest. He uses many things to come to our rescue and to comfort us. Sometimes all we can do is to get into the basket provided for us, be quiet, and trust the One holding the rope. Whether weak or strong, living dependently on Christ is the best way to live.

Questions to consider this week:

- In the midst of your most painful trial, how have you seen Jesus' grace be sufficient for you? How have you seen His power made complete in your weakness?

- When people mistake your love for something contrary to your true intentions, how do you tend to respond?

THE GOD-DEPENDENT WOMAN

DAY ONE STUDY—GET THE BIG PICTURE.

Ask the Lord Jesus to teach you through His Word.

Read the Bible passage below (NIV, including verses from the last lesson). Use your own method (colored pencils, lines, shapes) to mark 1) anything that grabs your attention, 2) words you want to understand, and 3) topics you have seen before in this letter. Draw arrows between thoughts that connect. Put a star ✸ next to anything you think relates to dependent living.

11 30 If I must boast, I will boast of the things that show my weakness. 31 The God and Father of the Lord Jesus, who is to be praised forever, knows that I am not lying. 32 In Damascus the governor under King Aretas had the city of the Damascenes guarded in order to arrest me. 33 But I was lowered in a basket from a window in the wall and slipped through his hands.

12 I must go on boasting. Although there is nothing to be gained, I will go on to visions and revelations from the Lord. 2 I know a man in Christ who fourteen years ago was caught up to the third heaven. Whether it was in the body or out of the body I do not know—God knows. 3 And I know that this man—whether in the body or apart from the body I do not know, but God knows— 4 was caught up to paradise and heard inexpressible things, things that no one is permitted to tell. 5 I will boast about a man like that, but I will not boast about myself, except about my weaknesses. 6 Even if I should choose to boast, I would not be a fool, because I would be speaking the truth. But I refrain, so no one will think more of me than is warranted by what I do or say, 7 or because of these surpassingly great revelations. Therefore, in order to keep me from becoming conceited, I was given a thorn in my flesh, a messenger of Satan, to torment me. 8 Three times I pleaded with the Lord to take it away from me. 9 But he said to me, "My grace is sufficient for you, for my power is made perfect in weakness." Therefore I will boast all the more gladly about my weaknesses, so that Christ's power may rest on me. 10 That is why, for Christ's sake, I delight in weaknesses, in insults, in hardships, in persecutions, in difficulties. For when I am weak, then I am strong.

11 I have made a fool of myself, but you drove me to it. I ought to have been commended by you, for I am not in the least inferior to the "super-apostles," even though I am nothing. 12 I persevered in demonstrating among you the marks of a true apostle, including signs, wonders and miracles. 13 How were you inferior to the other churches, except that I was never a burden to you? Forgive me this wrong!

14 Now I am ready to visit you for the third time, and I will not be a burden to you, because what I want is not your possessions but you. After all, children should not have to save up for their parents, but parents for their children. 15 So I will very gladly spend for you everything I have and expend myself as well. If I love you more, will you love me less? 16 Be that as it may, I have not been a burden to you. Yet, crafty fellow that I am, I caught you by trickery! 17 Did I exploit you through any of the men I sent to you? 18 I urged Titus to go to you and I sent our brother with him. Titus did not exploit you, did he? Did we not walk in the same footsteps by the same Spirit?

19 Have you been thinking all along that we have been defending ourselves to you? We have been speaking in the sight of God as those in Christ; and everything we do, dear friends, is for your strengthening. 20 For I am afraid that when I come I may not find you as I want you to be, and you may not find me as you want me to be. I fear that there may be discord, jealousy, fits of rage, selfish ambition, slander, gossip, arrogance and disorder. 21 I am afraid that when I come again my God will humble me before you, and I will be grieved over many who have sinned earlier and have not repented of the impurity, sexual sin and debauchery in which they have indulged.

LESSON TEN

1. What grabbed your attention from these verses?
   - 12:1-10

   - 12:11-18

   - 12:19-21

2. What verses or specific words do you want to understand better?

3. What topics are repeated in this passage or continue an earlier discussion in this letter?

4. What verses illustrate or help you understand what dependent living on God looks like?

Respond to the Lord about what He has shown you today.

THE GOD-DEPENDENT WOMAN

DAY TWO STUDY

Read 2 Corinthians 12:1-10. Ask the Lord Jesus to teach you through His Word.

What does the Bible say?

> **Focus on the Meaning:** The "third heaven" probably represents the presence of God. It could be a technical description of God's abode, above the cloudy heavens overhead, and beyond the farthest reaches of space that man can perceive. "Paradise" (v. 4) is a good synonym for the third heaven (cf. Luke 23:43; Revelation 2:7). (*Dr. Constable's Notes on 2 Corinthians 2017 Edition,* p. 116)

5. Paul shares his vision from Christ and what he learned from that experience.

   What happened 14 years before this letter was written (v. 2)?

   While in paradise (heaven), what did he hear (v. 4)?

   About what does he choose to boast rather than that experience (v. 5)?

   If he chooses to boast about that experience, he would not be a fool (liar) because it was true. Why does he refrain from boasting about that experience (v. 6)?

   In order to keep from being conceited, what happened (v. 7)?

   Three times, Paul did what (v. 8)?

   Write Jesus' answer to him (v. 9, first part) in the space below:

   What is Paul's response to Jesus (v. 9, second part)?

   Write Paul's choice of how to live his life (v. 10) in the space below:

LESSON TEN

Did anything else grab your attention?

> **Historical Insight:** Paul said he was caught up to heaven 14 years before the writing of this letter (56 AD). That would have happened around 42 AD. Paul was back in Tarsus ministering in Syria and Cilicia (Acts 9:30; Galatians 1:21). This was before Paul went to Antioch to pastor the church there and before he went on any missionary journey. No wonder he was so sure of his mission and his life knowing Christ.

What does it mean?

Looking at v. 6, we see that Paul preferred to be remembered for what he said and did in following Christ rather than for that one extraordinary experience that certainly contrasts with sneaking out of Damascus in a basket!

6. Why did Paul share this experience with the Corinthians after keeping it private for 14 years? See also v. 11 and 13:3.

> **Think About It:** We love the sensational. We get excited for a miracle or a good vision or dream. ... we're infatuated with the platforms of Christian celebrities ... But do we have the same level of passion for daily faithfulness? ... it's the consistent godly patterns of our lives that yield enduring fruit. (Kelly Minter, *All Things New*, p. 175)

7. Let's look at Paul's "thorn in the flesh." Although a lot of speculations are made, no one knows what this ailment was. Most of us can identify with having a thorn or splinter stuck in our skin at some point in our lives.

    - What does Paul mean by calling it a "thorn in his flesh" (v. 7)?

    - The Lord in His goodness allowed Satan to touch Paul's body with this "thorn" (as in Job 2:10). For what purpose?

    - Though this faithful follower of Christ pleaded three times for it to be removed, did Jesus remove it?

155

THE GOD-DEPENDENT WOMAN

8. To understand God's answer, read 2 Corinthians 12:9 in *The Message* and 2 other Bible translations then answer the questions below.

  - God said His grace is sufficient (most English translations use this word). Paul used a word (Gr. *arkeo*) that means, "to be possessed of unfailing strength, enough." Grace is God's provision for our every need when we need it. How can God's grace be sufficient when you have a persistent thorn?

  - God's power is made perfect in weakness. "Made perfect" means "perfected, finished, exactly fitting the need in a certain situation or purpose." Jesus said the same thing on the cross in John 19:30. See also 2 Corinthians 13:4. How is God's power made perfect in weakness?

9. After Paul heard from Jesus, his tone changed from pleading with the Lord to remove the thorn to what entirely new response (vv. 9-10)?

   From the Greek: The word translated "rest" referring to Christ's power means "to dwell, to take possession of and live in." The word translated "delight" means "seems good, take pleasure in, ready to do, think well of."

10. Why would Paul be willing to delight in (consider good, think well of) weaknesses, insults, hardships, persecutions and difficulties "for Christ's sake?"

11. Consider the 14 years since Paul's third heaven experience and all that he went through since that time. In what ways had Paul been made strong in weaknesses, insults, hardships, persecutions, and difficulties?

Scriptural Insight: Paul's response relates back to what he shared previously about his own life. Look back at Acts 18:9-11; 2 Corinthians 1:9; 4:7-11; 6:3-10 and 11:21-33.

11. Considering the definitions in the "From the Greek" above, how can it be that when you are weak (admit it, boast in it, even be glad about it), you are strong?

Think About It: God is attracted to weakness. He can't resist those who humbly and honestly admit how desperately they need Him. Our weakness, in fact, makes room for His power. (Jim Cymbala, *Fresh Wind, Fresh Fire*)

13. What else did you learn as you studied 2 Corinthians 12:1-10?

What application will you make?

14. What could it look like, feel like, and sound like (the words we use) if we applied vv. 9-10 to our lives?

15. In the midst of your most painful trial, how have you seen Christ's words to be true, "My grace is sufficient for you, for my power is made perfect in weakness?"

16. Have you been spending precious energy trying to solve or figure out "a thorn" in your life? If there doesn't appear to be a clear answer—or at least in the near future—take a moment to entrust it to the God who knows.

17. In what other ways can you apply this lesson to your life?

Respond to the Lord about what He has shown you today.

Consider using any creative means to respond to the Lord's grace being sufficient for your every weakness—poem, song, painting, craft, prose, or other means.

LESSON TEN

Day Three Study

Read 2 Corinthians 12:11-18. Ask the Lord Jesus to teach you through His Word.

What does the Bible say?

18. See how Paul picks up again on what he shared in 2 Corinthians 11:1-12 …

    I ought to have been _____ (v. 11) for I am not

    _____ even though I

    _____.

    What things mark an apostle that were done in Corinth (v. 12)?

    Why does Paul choose not to be a burden to them (v. 14)?

    Like parents do for their children, Paul says he will very gladly do what (v. 15, first part)?

    What illogical question does he ask (v. 15, second part)?

    What 3 questions did he ask them about himself and Titus (vv. 17-18)?

    Did anything else grab your attention?

What does it mean?

19. Focus on v. 11.

    - How was Paul "nothing" (no one, a nobody)? See also 2 Corinthians 10:10.

    - How does Paul's "nothing" relate to what you read in 2 Corinthians 11:30 and 12:9?

20. What does he confirm about his behavior toward them (vv. 14, 16-17)?

THE GOD-DEPENDENT WOMAN

21. Contrast the false teachers' behavior (11:19-21) with that of Paul and his associates. See also 2 Corinthians 7:13-16; 8:22-23.

False Teachers	Paul and his associates

22. What else did you learn as you studied 2 Corinthians 12:11-18?

> **Focus on the Meaning:** Paul's focusing on the signs (evidences) of an apostle, rather than on the rights of an apostle, is helpful for all servants of the Lord to observe. We, too, should concentrate on demonstrating the proofs of our ambassadorship in our works, especially our perseverance, rather than expecting those we serve to follow us because we are "claiming" our rights. We need to earn the respect of those we serve, with our works and by our example, rather than demanding it because of our position. (*Dr. Constable's Notes on 2 Corinthians 2017 Edition*, p. 121)

What application will you make?

23. When people mistake your love for something else (especially contrary to your true intentions), that can be deeply wounding. Is that something you are experiencing right now or have experienced in the past? Look at Paul's response in today's passage. What can you learn from him that challenges and inspires you for dealing with this hurtful experience?

24. In what other ways can you apply this lesson to your life?

Respond to the Lord about what He has shown you today.

LESSON TEN

Day Four Study

Read 2 Corinthians 12:19-21. Ask the Lord Jesus to teach you through His Word.

What does the Bible say?

25. Paul had genuine concerns (fears) about his next visit to the church. Fear is a normal human emotion designed by God to alert us to danger so that we can take action against it. Answer the following questions based on what is in the biblical text.

    Who does Paul say is a witness to his words (v. 19; 11:31)?

    What does he call them in v. 19? See also 7:1.

    Everything he does is for what purpose (v. 19)?

    What are his fears about visiting them (v. 20, second part)?

    What also might happen when he visits them (v. 21)?

    In what had some of them been indulging (v. 21)?

    Did anything else grab your attention?

    Focus on the Meaning: The phrase "God will humble me before you is explained in the rest of v. 21. Grieving over the failures of his spiritual children will bring him humiliation. The Corinthians' failure to repent had embarrassed him on his former painful visit (2 Corinthians 2:1-4). The list of sins here reflects a church in turmoil. Paul as an apostle has authority over them to call out and correct their sinful behavior.

What does it mean?

26. What could Paul mean by saying "you may find me not as you want me to be?" See 10:10-11 and 13:10.

27. What else did you learn as you studied 2 Corinthians 12:19-21?

What application will you make?

What Paul describes in v. 20 sounds like some family gatherings, especially around the holidays. Does it sound familiar to you?

28. Describe a time when you had anxiety over seeing someone you hadn't seen in a while. What were your worries? How did you prepare yourself? Did it go as you expected or were you surprised?

29. The sinful behaviors Paul mentions in vv. 20-21 are common to humans. Paul mentions these same things in most of his other letters. See Galatians 5:19-21, Ephesians 4:25-32; 5:3-4, and Colossians 3:5-10 for example. Are you "indulging" in any of these behaviors? If so, purify yourself now (2 Corinthians 7:1). See Lesson 6, Day Four Study application for the biblical process for dealing with sin in your life. Repentance begins with *agreeing* with God that what you are doing is sin against Him. *Mourn* your behavior because it causes Him sadness. *Commit* to letting the Spirit transform you in that area of your life (2 Corinthians 3:17-18). *Trust* Him to work in and through you beginning today.

30. In what other ways can you apply this lesson to your life?

LESSON TEN

31. Review the passage for this lesson in "Day One Study." Add reasons why God wants us to depend on Him more than on ourselves to the chart below. I have given a few prompts.

Verse(s)	Reasons why God wants us to depend on Him more than on ourselves
12:6	*To refrain from boasting about personal spiritual experiences*
12:7-8	*Enduring a thorn in the flesh that God chooses not to heal*
12:9	*Trusting God's grace to be sufficient*
12:9	*Being glad about weaknesses so Christ's power shines*

Respond to the Lord about what He has shown you today.

As His child, God transforms your life by teaching you to live dependently on Him in weakness and in strength.

Recommended: Listen to "God's Grace Is Sufficient" to reinforce what you have learned. Use the following listener guide.

PODCAST LISTENER GUIDE

God's Grace Is Sufficient

DEPENDENT LIVING IS HARD.

- Paul kept that "third heaven" experience to himself all those years and refrained from boasting about that experience. Christ gave him the ability to do that."

- God gave him an ongoing thorn in the flesh to keep him from being conceited about having this personal experience. On his knees, Paul listened to Christ say "no" to removing the thorn and give him the reason for doing so. "My grace is sufficient for you, for my power is made perfect in weakness." So, Paul basically said, "Hooray for my weaknesses. I want Christ and His power on me more than my own. For when I am weak, then I am strong." Who can do that on their own? No one! Christ gave him the ability to do that.

- All our physical ailments are not from Satan. Most of the time they're from living in a fallen world where sin has caused disease and destruction. A thorn is anything that drives us to God, making us weak so we have to depend on Him. The truth is that the thorn experiences make us more usable towards God's purposes than the "third heaven" ones do. Christ not only permitted all those hardships in Paul's life but had purpose in doing so.

- Dependent living is hard. It is refraining from boasting about spiritual experiences. It is enduring a thorn in the flesh God chooses not to heal. It is trusting God's grace to be sufficient to handle anything in life. It is being glad about weaknesses so Christ's power shines in you instead of your own. It is trusting Him for strength all the time, not just when you can't do something on your own. It is spending yourself for others so they grow spiritually. It is doing everything in the sight of God, through Christ, and for the strengthening of other believers around us. It is also being humbled by God before others so they see Christ more than you. And it is being grieved by unrepentant sin in those around you.

GOD'S GRACE IS SUFFICIENT.

- When Christ said to Paul that His grace was sufficient, He used a word meaning "to be possessed of unfailing strength, to be enough." God's grace is His unmerited favor toward humans. It is a gift from God that we don't deserve and can never earn.

    ✓ Salvation by faith alone through Christ alone is a gift of God's grace.
    ✓ The Holy Spirit's presence in every believer as a deposit guaranteeing our future inheritance of a perfected body and soul is a gift of God's grace.
    ✓ Being transformed into the likeness of Christ during this earthly life of ours is a gift of God's grace.
    ✓ All those wonderful treasures that come to us as new creations in Christ are gifts of God's grace. They are enough to make us into whatever God purposes for us to be. God's protection and deliverance from deadly peril are gifts of God's grace.
    ✓ Every healing. Every answer to prayer. Every time we get guidance about what to do and where to go. Those are gifts of God's grace. They are sufficient to get us through this life and have joy in the process.

- ✓ The power of Christ working in us to help us in our weakness so that we can say with Paul, "I will boast all the more gladly about my weaknesses, so that Christ's power may rest on me." That is a gift of God's grace.

- When you admit that you are weak, you desire Christ's power to rest on you. That means to take possession of you, to act on your behalf. It is a heart change when you desire more of Him and less of yourself.

- As the years passed, Paul relied more on Christ so Christ showed through him. The Holy Spirit made sure we could see that, too. Paul wanted those looking at his life to see how to follow Christ so that they would do it, too. He didn't do everything right. Neither will we. God's gift of grace covers our mistakes as well.

- Christ's power made perfect in weakness is what He did on the cross for us! It is what He wants to do in us and through us.

  Jesus Christ gave His life *for* you, so He could give His life *to* you, so He could live His life *through* you. (Major Ian Thomas, T*he Saving Life of Christ*)

- His grace is sufficient to save us. It is sufficient to regenerate our dead spirits so that we are spiritually alive for eternity. And it is sufficient to live His life through us as we let Him. God transforms your life by teaching you to live dependently on Him in weakness and in strength. You learn how to do this as you act in obedience to the Word of God, depend on Jesus Christ for the power to do so, and trust Him with the results. This "dependent living" will make you stronger and more effective in life as you become a God-dependent woman.

IS DEPENDING ON GOD ACKNOWLEDGING HIS STRENGTH?

True or False? *"Depending on God isn't a weakness ... It is acknowledging His strength. The more we depend on God the more dependable we find He is."* **TRUE**

This is actually a true saying. Dependent living isn't weakness. We do acknowledge His strength when we choose to depend on Him. The more we do so, the more we personally discover how truly dependable He is and has been all along. Win/win.

REASONS WHY GOD WANTS US TO DEPEND ON HIM MORE THAN ON OURSELVES

- ✓ To refrain from boasting about personal spiritual experiences. (12:6)
- ✓ Enduring a thorn in the flesh that God chooses not to heal. (12:7-8)
- ✓ Trusting God's grace to be sufficient. (12:9)
- ✓ Being glad about weaknesses so Christ's power shines. (12:9)
- ✓ Trusting Him for strength. (12:10)
- ✓ To love others so much you don't want to "use" them in any way. (12:14)
- ✓ To spend ourselves for others to grow spiritually. (12:15, 19)
- ✓ To walk by the Spirit consistently with other believers. (12:17)
- ✓ Facing sin in those we love. (12:20-21)

Let Jesus satisfy your heart with confidence that you can depend on Him. Then, live each day as a God-dependent woman!

11: Christ Is All We Need for Life

2 Corinthians 13:1-14

...since you are demanding proof that Christ is speaking through me. He is not weak in dealing with you, but is powerful among you. For to be sure, he was crucified in weakness, yet he lives by God's power. Likewise, we are weak in him, yet by God's power we will live with him in our dealing with you. (2 Corinthians 13:3-4)

As we have studied this letter, 2 Corinthians, we have seen how personal and messy it is. It is messy because it is full of emotions and experiences. It is like life—messy—because people are messy, relationships are messy, circumstances are messy, and community within the church is messy.

In the midst of our messy lives, God wants us to learn to rely on Him more than on ourselves. Throughout 2 Corinthians, we have seen examples of Paul making plans and submitting them to God to be changed, demonstrating his authority and submitting that to God, asking for healing and submitting to God's answer, and preaching the gospel in one city while his heart wants to be in another city but waits for God to say "go." That is dependent living.

Through your study of 2 Corinthians, you have learned how the Lord Jesus Christ will transform your life as His child by teaching you to live dependently on Him in weakness and in strength. This "dependent living" will lead to you becoming stronger and more effective in life by relying on God rather than on yourself. You learn how to do this as you act according to the Word of God, depend on Jesus Christ for the power to do so, and trust Him with the results.

He is all you need to find the best way to live!

Questions to consider this week:

- What is the proof of Jesus' hand on our lives?
- Why is it necessary to lovingly confront someone you love about their sin? What is the goal of doing so?

THE GOD-DEPENDENT WOMAN

DAY ONE STUDY—GET THE BIG PICTURE.

Ask the Lord Jesus to teach you through His Word.

Read the Bible passage below (NIV, including verses from the last lesson). Use your own method (colored pencils, lines, shapes) to mark 1) anything that grabs your attention, 2) words you want to understand, and 3) topics you have seen before in this letter. Draw arrows between thoughts that connect. Put a star ✻ next to anything you think relates to dependent living.

12 14 Now I am ready to visit you for the third time, and I will not be a burden to you, because what I want is not your possessions but you. After all, children should not have to save up for their parents, but parents for their children. 15 So I will very gladly spend for you everything I have and expend myself as well. If I love you more, will you love me less? 16 Be that as it may, I have not been a burden to you. Yet, crafty fellow that I am, I caught you by trickery! 17 Did I exploit you through any of the men I sent to you? 18 I urged Titus to go to you and I sent our brother with him. Titus did not exploit you, did he? Did we not walk in the same footsteps by the same Spirit?

19 Have you been thinking all along that we have been defending ourselves to you? We have been speaking in the sight of God as those in Christ; and everything we do, dear friends, is for your strengthening. 20 For I am afraid that when I come I may not find you as I want you to be, and you may not find me as you want me to be. I fear that there may be discord, jealousy, fits of rage, selfish ambition, slander, gossip, arrogance and disorder. 21 I am afraid that when I come again my God will humble me before you, and I will be grieved over many who have sinned earlier and have not repented of the impurity, sexual sin and debauchery in which they have indulged.

13 This will be my third visit to you. "Every matter must be established by the testimony of two or three witnesses." 2 I already gave you a warning when I was with you the second time. I now repeat it while absent: On my return I will not spare those who sinned earlier or any of the others, 3 since you are demanding proof that Christ is speaking through me. He is not weak in dealing with you, but is powerful among you. 4 For to be sure, he was crucified in weakness, yet he lives by God's power. Likewise, we are weak in him, yet by God's power we will live with him in our dealing with you.

5 Examine yourselves to see whether you are in the faith; test yourselves. Do you not realize that Christ Jesus is in you—unless, of course, you fail the test? 6 And I trust that you will discover that we have not failed the test. 7 Now we pray to God that you will not do anything wrong—not so that people will see that we have stood the test but so that you will do what is right even though we may seem to have failed. 8 For we cannot do anything against the truth, but only for the truth. 9 We are glad whenever we are weak but you are strong; and our prayer is that you may be fully restored. 10 This is why I write these things when I am absent, that when I come I may not have to be harsh in my use of authority—the authority the Lord gave me for building you up, not for tearing you down.

11 Finally, brothers and sisters, rejoice! Strive for full restoration, encourage one another, be of one mind, live in peace. And the God of love and peace will be with you.

12 Greet one another with a holy kiss. 13 All God's people here send their greetings.

14 May the grace of the Lord Jesus Christ, and the love of God, and the fellowship of the Holy Spirit be with you all.

LESSON ELEVEN

1. What grabbed your attention from these verses?
    - 13:1-4

    - 13:5-10

    - 13:11-14

2. What verses or specific words do you want to understand better?

3. What topics are repeated in this passage or continue an earlier discussion in this letter?

4. What verses illustrate or help you understand what dependent living on God looks like?

Respond to the Lord about what He has shown you today.

THE GOD-DEPENDENT WOMAN

Day Two Study

Read 2 Corinthians 13:1-4. Ask the Lord Jesus to teach you through His Word.

What does the Bible say?

5. Paul continues his discussion of his planned visit to the Corinthians.

    In v. 1, Paul quotes Deuteronomy 19:15. What does the Bible say?

    On his visit to Corinth, what will Paul do (v. 2)?

    What were they demanding (v. 3, first part)?

    What does he tell them in response (v. 3, second part)?

    What is true about Christ (v. 4, first part)? Note: Christ illustrated 2 Corinthians 12:9 for us.

    What is likewise true about Paul and his leader team (v. 4, second part)?

    Did anything else grab your attention?

    > **Focus on the Meaning:** What did Paul mean by the "two or three witnesses?" He could be referring to himself, Titus, and the other brother when they last visited the Corinthians. Or it could be the people who know the truth about Paul, heard the warning from him before, and will be present when he comes to visit the church.

What does it mean?

6. Paul takes his authority and responsibility of servant-leadership in the church very seriously. Summarize what he is saying to the Corinthians.

    > **Scriptural Insight:** Rebellion against Paul is rebellion against Christ, who appointed him as His apostle. (*NIV Study Bible,* note on 13:3, p. 1777)

LESSON ELEVEN

7. Does God's power (v. 4) shown through His representatives include the authority to judge sin and correct sinful behavior in Christians? See v. 10 and 2 Corinthians 2:5-10; 6:14-7:1; 7:8-13; 11:3-4; and 12:20-21 to help you answer this question.

Focus on the Meaning: It appears that Paul and the Corinthians did not understand "power" in the same way. For them it was on display in an aggressive and a mighty personality. For the apostle, it is seen in weakness [that relies on Christ]. *(Dr. Constable's Notes on 2 Corinthians 2017 Edition,* p. 124)

8. What else did you learn as you studied 2 Corinthians 13:1-4?

Scriptural Insight: Christ's finished work on the cross is His power perfected for us. See the podcast notes after Lessons 5 and 6 for description of some of what He made complete for us.

What application will you make?

9. Is the proof of Jesus' hand on our lives found only in big money, big deals, flashes of fame, and our biggest dreams coming true? If not, why not? Use what you have learned in this letter to explain your answer.

Think About It: Dear follower of Christ, make sure you're not judging the proof of God's hand on your life merely by outward, materialistic blessings. As we've seen throughout 2 Corinthians, oftentimes His greatest display of power in our lives is in our places of loneliness, battles with infirmities, and painful losses. Whether you're feeling weak or strong, hide yourself as weak in Christ. A child is weak when resting in her father's arms. This is where we'll find the true strength to love God and serve others. (Kelly Minter, *All Things New,* p. 200)

10. In what other ways can you apply this lesson to your life?

Respond to the Lord about what He has shown you today.

THE GOD-DEPENDENT WOMAN

DAY THREE STUDY

Read 2 Corinthians 13:5-10. Ask the Lord Jesus to teach you through His Word.

What does the Bible say?

11. Answer the following questions based on the text.

    Paul says the Corinthians should examine (or test) themselves to see that they are in the faith. As someone in the faith, what is true about them and you (v. 5)?

    What does Paul say about himself (v. 6)?

    What is his prayer for them (v. 7)?

    What does he confirm in v. 8?

    On what is Paul's focus as he exercises authority over the Corinthians (v. 9)?

    Why does he write such seemingly harsh words to them (v. 10, first part)?

    Why did Jesus give him authority (v. 10, second part)?

    Did anything else grab your attention?

What does it mean?

> **From the Greek:** Paul meant v. 5 to be an affirming question, carrying the idea of "proving in the expectation of approving." The Greek word *peirazo* means "to try, make trial of, test: for the purpose of ascertaining quality, or one's thinking, or how one will behave himself." The end result is to show that what one expected is true. The Corinthians had been examining him. Now he turned the tables and challenged them to examine themselves—not for salvation but for obedience to the Lord.

12. Paul wanted the Corinthians to take a hard look at themselves with the expectation they would discover that Jesus Christ was truly in their lives and working in their midst. What evidence would show this to be true? [They would only fail the test if they had never trusted in Christ.]

LESSON ELEVEN

From the Greek: The end of verse 9 reads very differently among the various translations. You will see "become mature" (NLT), "fully qualified" (NET), "made complete" (NAS), and "fully restored" (NIV, ESV). You will see the same differences in verse 11. The Greek words used there carry the idea of strengthening, perfecting, training, being completely ready to take on whatever is needed. The goal is to move forward in your transformation to become more like Jesus Christ and serve Him well.

13. Relate v. 9 to what you learned in 2 Corinthians 12. What could Paul have meant when he said he is glad when he is weak and the Corinthians are fully restored or made complete?

14. What is the proper use of authority in the church (v. 10)? See also 2 Corinthians 1:24 and 10:8.

What application will you make?

15. Why is it necessary to lovingly confront someone you love about their sin? What is the goal of doing so?

Respond to the Lord about what He has shown you today.

Notice Paul's mention of prayer twice in this section. Every daily lesson in this study begins and ends with prayer. Lack of prayer is often a sign of self-sufficiency rather than dependent living and will lead you to doing what is not pleasing in God's sight. **Spend some time responding to the Lord about what He has shown you today**.

THE GOD-DEPENDENT WOMAN

Day Four Study

Read 2 Corinthians 13:11-14. Ask the Lord Jesus to teach you through His Word.

What does the Bible say?

16. Paul's closing words in a letter often include simple reminders of how to live as a Christian in community. As he says goodbye, Paul sums up his letter with five "take-away" actions in v. 11. What are they?

What does it mean?

17. What does Paul mean when he tells them to strive or aim for full restoration (NIV, ESV)? To what or whom must they be restored? See also 2 Corinthians 11:3 and 12:20-21.

> **Historical Insight:** Evidently Paul's anticipated visit to Corinth turned out to be a pleasant one. Paul wrote Romans during the three months he was in Corinth (Acts 20:2-3, A.D. 56-57). In that epistle, he gave no indication that there were problems in Corinth. Moreover, he proceeded with his plans to evangelize unreached areas, which he would not have done if the Corinthian church still needed his attention (cf. 2 Corinthians 10:14-16). Furthermore, Paul wrote that the believers in Achaia (includes the Corinthians) "were pleased" to complete their collection for the Jerusalem saints (Romans 15:26-27). Finally, the Corinthian church's preservation of 2 Corinthians argues for this church's acquiescence to Paul's admonitions and warnings. (*Dr. Constable's Notes on 2 Corinthians 2017 Edition*, p. 127)

18. Focus on the phrases: "be of one mind" and "live in peace." You can find "cross references" (verses that are similar to the one you are reading) in most study Bibles and in the Blue Letter Bible App. Look at cross references to find other verses that describe how to:

    - be of one mind—

    - live in peace—

LESSON ELEVEN

Historical Insight: The "holy kiss (v. 12)" was an expression of brotherly love, a sign of being in fellowship with one another. It welcomed newly baptized believers into the family of God. It symbolized the forgiveness, reconciliation, unity, and fellowship that existed between the believers.

19. Write Paul's benediction (v. 14) in the space below.

20. What do you learn about the three persons of our one God from this verse?

Scriptural Insight: This benediction confirms the Trinity and has ever since been a part of Christian worship tradition. It serves to remind us that the mystery of the Holy Trinity is known to be true not through rational or philosophical explanations but through Christian experience, whereby the believer knows firsthand the grace, the love, and the fellowship that freely flow to him from the three Persons of the one Lord God. (*NIV Study Bible*, note on v. 14, p. 1778)

What application will you make?

21. Review the passage for this lesson in "Day One Study." Add reasons why God wants us to depend on Him more than on ourselves to the chart below. I have given a few prompts.

Verse(s)	Reasons why God wants us to depend on Him more than on ourselves
13:4	To live by God's power to deal with people
13:5	To gain assurance that you are in Christ by your faith in Him
13:7	For our disciples to do what is right even though we may fail
13:8	To stand for the truth

THE GOD-DEPENDENT WOMAN

> Check out the chart "Why Depend on God More than on Yourself" in the RESOURCES section for the reasons to depend on God that I discovered in 2 Corinthians. Add any others you discovered to the list.

FAMOUS LAST WORDS

What are your takeaways from this study? What have you learned about being a God-dependent woman? Have you learned to depend on Christ more? In what ways do you understand dependent living better? Are you making the choices daily to live in God-dependency rather than self-sufficiency?

Respond to the Lord about what He has shown you today.

As His child, God transforms your life by teaching you to live dependently on Him in weakness and in strength.

> **Recommended:** Listen to "Jesus Satisfies Your Heart with Himself" to reinforce what you have learned. Use the following listener guide.

LESSON ELEVEN

PODCAST LISTENER GUIDE

Jesus Satisfies Your Heart with Himself

A relationship with another human cannot satisfy a spiritually thirsty heart. Only God can. His plan to do that included coming to earth to take on a human body and live as a human among us. Enter Jesus, the one who demonstrated God's love for women.

JESUS DEMONSTRATED GOD'S LOVE FOR WOMEN.

- Jesus Christ entered into the midst of His Jewish culture, influenced by Greek and Roman traditions, with a radically different value system in the way He regarded women. His compassion for women elevated their position in society and gave them equal relationship with Him.
    - ✓ Jesus spoke to women publicly when a rabbi wouldn't speak publicly to his wife.
    - ✓ Jesus let them travel with Him during His public ministry and support Him with their own money.
    - ✓ He taught women openly and continually when the rabbis didn't consider them able to be educated.
    - ✓ Jesus defended them when they were criticized.
    - ✓ He was sensitive and compassionate toward them and healed their loved ones.
    - ✓ Jesus made them the first witnesses to His resurrection when women were considered to be unreliable as witnesses.

- Jesus never spoke condescendingly to women, never made derogatory jokes about them, nor did he ever humiliate them. Women who knew Him loved Him, wanted to follow and serve Him! [See Live Out His Love and Satisfied by His Love Bible Studies for more on this.]

- His warmth, personal attention, tenderness, sound teaching, and compassion toward women were revolutionary. And why shouldn't He be compassionate toward women? Jesus is fully God. He created us and is the one who understands women.

JESUS IS THE ONE WHO UNDERSTANDS WOMEN.

- As Creator, **He designed us with a mind to know God, emotions to love God, and a will to obey God**. We are designed with a mind to know God, emotions to love God, and a will to obey God. That comes in the package we receive at birth.

- Our female minds need to be filled with the knowledge of Him so that our hearts may respond with great love for Him, and our wills can choose to obey Him.

- Jesus knows us backwards and forwards. He knows our emotional nature, our need for security and significance, and even our hormones! He understands our need to nurture and to be loved—both from those humans closest to us and from our Creator God.

- **Here's a key truth I want you to grasp.** A relationship with Jesus satisfies every spiritual need that you have. Every single one of them. You don't need to go anywhere else to get those deep needs satisfied.

JESUS IS THE ONE WHO MEETS YOUR SPIRITUAL NEEDS

> *"Praise the Lord, my soul, and forget not all His benefits—who forgives all your sins and heals all your diseases, who redeems your life from the pit and crowns you with love and compassion, who **satisfies your desires with good things** so that your youth is renewed like the eagle's." (Psalm 103:2-5)*

- Do you need forgiveness? Jesus does that. Do you need healing and hope for dire circumstances? Jesus does that. Do you feel like you are in spiritual bondage? Jesus can set you free from that. Do you need assurance that you are loved? Jesus crowns you with His love and compassion. To be crowned with compassion means to be surrounded with it so that you have a sense of God's favor and protection. A satisfied heart can go forward with complete assurance that our God knows how to love you well!

- God promises to satisfy your heart's desires with good things. You will be so satisfied that you will feel renewed and released to soar like an eagle. And He fills us with everything we need to feel satisfied.

- Our God created us with a spiritual thirst for a relationship with Him. A relationship with another human cannot satisfy that thirst. Jesus Christ satisfies your thirsty heart.

DO WE PRAY AS IF EVERYTHING DEPENDED ON GOD OR US?

True or False? *"Pray as if everything depended on God. Work as if everything depended on you."* **FALSE**

When you work like it depends on you and pray like it depends on God, it's too easy to start taking credit for the work you do. Or your efforts fail and you blame yourself for not working hard enough. Or others blame you for not working hard enough.

The two aspects of trusting God are this: The first one is that you must depend on Him as you step forward and do your part His way. The second aspect is that you must trust Him to do His part in the areas over which you have no control. So, getting back to our saying, it leaves out the trusting God while you are working to do your part His way. This saying is not good advice.

REASONS WHY GOD WANTS US TO DEPEND ON HIM MORE THAN ON OURSELVES

- ✓ To live by God's power to deal with people. (13:4)
- ✓ To gain assurance that you are in Christ by your faith in Him. (13:5)
- ✓ For our disciples to do what is right even though we may fail. (13:7)
- ✓ To stand for the truth. (13:8)
- ✓ To be fully restored/matured in pure devotion to Christ. (13:9)
- ✓ To be concerned for disciples' growth more than your own personal reputation. (13:7, 9)
- ✓ To build others up and not tear them down. (13:10)
- ✓ To rejoice, mature, encourage others, be united, and live in peace with other believers. (13:11)

Let Jesus satisfy your heart with confidence that you can depend on Him. Then, live each day as a God-dependent woman!

RESOURCES

Why Depend on God More than on Yourself

What Paul teaches us in 2 Corinthians

The Reasons Why We Should Depend on God	2 Corinthians
We receive comfort from God for ourselves and to comfort others	1:4
He is more powerful than we are	1:9
We set our hope on Him to deliver us	1:10
He graciously answers our prayers	1:11
He is faithful to His promises	1:20
He owns us and lives in us	1:22
We get distracted and disappointed when things don't go as we plan	1:17
To reconcile relationships rightly when our feelings are hurt	2:1-10
To execute tough love when a Christian is deliberately sinning	2:5-10
To keep Satan from getting an advantage over us	2:11
He uses us to spread the knowledge of Him	2:14
He sends us to speak for Him	2:17
He writes a letter of recommendation for Himself in our lives	3:3
He gives us confidence to trust Him	3:4
He gives us competence to represent Him	3:5
He takes away the veil over our hearts when we believe	3:16
He transforms us by His Spirit	3:18
To not lose heart	4:1
He makes His light shine in the darkness through us	4:6
He can demonstrate His power through our frailty (jars of clay)	4:7
He keeps us from being crushed when we are burdened	4:8-9
He reveals Jesus' life in and through us	4:10
He will give us a new resurrection/heavenly body as a reward	4:14; 5:1; 5:5
He can keep us from losing heart	4:16
He renews us inwardly while we outwardly "waste away"	4:16
He gives us an eternal perspective about our "light, momentary troubles"	4:18
Because we must live by faith not by sight	5:7
We will be with Him when this life ends	5:8
To learn how to live to please Him	5:9
He rewards us for our earthly lives	5:10

To live for Him rather than for ourselves	5:15
He has made us into a new creation	5:17
We are His ambassadors and speak for Him	5:19-20
He exchanges our sin for Christ's righteousness	5:21
We are His servants	6:4
To respond to troubles in a godly manner	6:4-9
Our lives influence others	6:10
We are His children	6:16-18
To purify ourselves to perfect holiness	7:1
He comforts us when we are downcast	7:6
To rightly respond to sin in our lives	7:9
To see truth in ourselves, in our hearts	7:12
He initiates the grace of giving	8:1
We need Him to direct our giving according to His will	8:5
He makes us spiritually rich so we can give	8:9
He puts into our hearts concerns for us to have	8:16
We are His representatives who honor Christ so can be trusted with money handling	8:23
God blesses us so we can give to others	9:8
God enlarges the harvest of our generosity and good works	9:10
God gives through us to meet the needs of His people	9:12
To treat others with the humility and gentleness of Christ	10:1
We need His power to demolish strongholds holding us captive	10:3-4
We need His power to take captive our thoughts for Him	10:5
To use our authority to build others up and not tear them down	10:8; 13:10
To find our sphere of service He has assigned to us	10:13
To confine our boasting to the Lord and the sphere of service He has assigned to us	10:13
To seek our approval and commendation from Him rather than others	10:17
To keep us from being led astray by false teaching	11:3
To help us recognize error in teaching	11:4-5
To know the truth about God	11:6
For financial support that enables us to share Christ and disciple others	11:7-9
To show us those masquerading as His servants and release us from their grip	11:13-15
To rescue us from danger	11:23-27; 32-33
To teach us the value of boasting about the things that show our weakness and need for Him	11:30
To keep praising God in all our afflictions	11:31

To help us handle the daily pressures of that which concerns us	11:28
To refrain from boasting about personal spiritual experiences	12:6
Enduring a thorn in the flesh that God chooses not to heal	12:7-8
Trusting God's grace to be sufficient	12:9
Being glad about weaknesses so Christ's power shines in us	12:9
Trusting Him for strength	12:10
To love others so much you don't want to "use" them in any way	12:14
To spend ourselves for others to grow spiritually	12:15, 19
To walk by the Spirit consistently with other believers	12:17
Facing sin in those we love	12:20-21
To live by God's power to deal with people	13:4
To gain assurance that you are in Christ by your faith in Him	13:5
For our disciples to do what is right even though we may fail	13:7
To stand for the truth	13:8
To be fully restored/matured in pure devotion to Christ	13:9
To be concerned for disciples' growth more than your own personal reputation	13:7, 9
To rejoice, mature, encourage others, be united, and live in peace with other believers	13:11

Ways to Explain the Gospel

EVANTELL.ORG

Has anyone ever taken a Bible and shown you how you can know you're going to heaven? May I?

- The Bible contains both bad news and good news. The bad news is something about you and me, and the good news is something about God. Let's discuss the bad news first.

  Bad News #1 — We are all sinners. *Romans 3:23*

  Bad News #2—The penalty for sin is death. *Romans 6:23*

- Since there was no way you could come to God, the Bible says that God decided to come to you.

  Good News #1—Christ died for you. *Romans 5:8*

  Good News #2—You can be saved through faith in Christ. *Ephesians 2:8-9*

- Is there anything keeping you from trusting Christ right now? Would you like to pray right now and tell God you are trusting His Son as your Savior?

You can watch a free online training video at http://evantell.org.

BRIDGE TO LIFE (NAVIGATORS)

- The Bible teaches that God loves all humans and wants them to know him. *John 10:10; Romans 5:1*
- But humans have sinned against God and are separated from God and his love. *Draw a chasm.* This separation leads only to death and judgment. *Romans 3:23; Isaiah 59:2*
- But there is a solution. *Draw bridge.* Jesus Christ died on the cross for our sins (the bridge between humanity and God). *1 Peter 3:18; 1 Timothy 2:5; Romans 5:8*
- Only those who personally receive Jesus Christ into their lives, trusting him to forgive their sins, can cross this bridge. Everyone must decide individually whether to receive Christ. *John 3:16; John 5:24*

FOUR SPIRITUAL LAWS (CRU)

- God loves you and offers a wonderful plan for your life. *John 3:16; 10:10*
- Humans are sinful and separated from God. Thus, they cannot know and experience God's love and plan for their lives. *Romans 3:23; Romans 6:23*
- Jesus Christ is God's only provision for humanity's sin. Through Jesus, you can know and experience God's love and plan for your life. *Romans 5:8; John 14:6*
- We must individually receive Jesus Christ as Savior and Lord, and then we can know and experience God's love and plan for our lives. *John 1:12; Ephesians 2:8-9*

  You can access this online at www.godlife.com.

USING JOHN 3:16

"For God so loved the world that he gave his one and only Son, that whoever believes in him shall not perish but have eternal life."

"Has anyone introduced you to Jesus so you could know Him? May I?"

- **God loves** — God is real. He loves you with an unconditional, never-ending love. ***"For God loves you** _____ (name) **so much…"*** He created you to have a relationship with Him. But we cannot experience this loving personal relationship because of sin in our lives. Sin is disobeying God. It puts a barrier between us and a holy God. No matter how hard you try, you cannot be good enough on your own to overcome this sin barrier. The penalty for sin is death. But God's love had a plan…

- **God gave** — "**God gave His one and only Son**" *Jesus* – to live as a human without sin and then to take the penalty for our sin on himself when he died on the cross. He was buried as a dead man then raised from the dead to be alive again. He did this so that our sins could be forgiven.

- **We believe God's love** — "**Whoever believes in Him**" – Faith is trust. God asks that we trust in His plan, admit our sin and desire for a relationship with Him. Accept what Jesus did on the cross for us out of love.

- **We receive what God gave** — "**Shall not perish but have eternal life**" – Everyone dies and ends up somewhere. To perish means to die separated from God and His love for you. Eternal life means you can enjoy a forever-family relationship with God and promise of living securely with Him now and after your life on earth ends.

- When offered a gift you want, you take it and say thank you. It is forever yours. Is there anything keeping you from trusting in Jesus right now?

DISCUSSION GUIDE

Small Group Discussion Guide

The following guide is designed for groups that meet for about 1½ hours or less. You will notice that some questions are skipped for the sake of time. These are only suggestions for you.

IF YOU HAVE A SEPARATE WEEK TO INTRODUCE THE STUDY:

- *Ask the group to listen to the first podcast "The Call to Dependent Living" before coming to the first meeting.* Send them a link to melanienewton.com/podcasts. Go to Series 8: 2 Corinthians.

Introduce the study

- Start with prayer. Pray for the group to learn from Jesus what He wants them to know and to learn to love one another well to build our community.

- Make sure everyone has a book, a schedule, and Bible / Bible app and knows how to use it. Ask if anyone is new to the Bible and plan to come alongside her during the week.

- Get acquainted with each other. Ask a general question or two such as, "Share your name, where you live, and an activity you enjoy when you have time to do so."

- **Pray:** Ask Jesus to teach you through this semester what He wants you to know. Ask Him to help you learn how to rely on Him more than on yourselves every day.

- **Introduction on Page 1**. Read the top paragraphs and "The Basic Study" section. Draw their attention to the useful study tools at the bottom of the page.

- **Look at Lesson 2** to illustrate how the lesson is arranged. First page has key verse, short review, and questions to consider that will come up again in the application questions. Every study day begins and ends in prayer. Day One Study is always observation of the whole passage. Starred questions illustrate dependent living. Opportunities are given throughout the lesson for you to add your own insights that are not covered by the questions. The chart at the end reviews the reasons for being God-dependent women.

- **Back to page 2**: Tell them how to find the podcasts (melanienewton.com/podcasts or any podcast platform—search "Satisfied" by Melanie Newton, Season 8). Or you can read the blogs associated with the podcasts at melanienewton.com/blog. Choose 2 Corinthians category then scroll to find the title you want. Read "New Testament Summary" or suggest they do so on their own. Read "Discussion Group Guidelines." Add anything else pertinent to your group.

- **The Call to Dependent Living Podcast:** Read and discuss the listener guide on pages 11-12. Ask questions and add insights based on your notes from listening to the podcast ahead of time. Discuss the questions asked in the third bullet point under "About Paul." This would work well in smaller groups of 2-4. Give them 5-minutes in small groups then have open sharing with the larger group.

- **Memory verses:** Tell the women to ask the Lord to help them memorize the specific verses recommended in Lesson One, page 16. Work on these together as a group.

- Tell them to work on Lesson One for the next meeting. Share prayer requests and pray for one another.

Recommendation: Listen to a worship song such as "Lord, I Need You."

Lesson 1: The God on Whom We Can Rely

Choose ahead of time which verses from the questions the group will read aloud as you proceed through the discussion. My recommendations are below.

Start with prayer.

- If you have not already discussed "The Call to Dependent Living" podcast, do so here. See suggestions above.

Day One Study

- Read Memory Verse #1 together at top of page. Skip reading the ABC's. Ask Q1.
- Skip reading the "The God-Dependent Woman and Dependent Living" section if you discussed the first podcast. Point out the memory verses. Ask Q2.

Day Two Study

- Highlight the importance of observation. Ask Q3.

Day Three Study

- Read the passage in sections. Qs4-5. Skip Q6.
- *What does the Bible say:* Ask Q7. Skip "Historical Insight."
- *What does it mean:* Read 1 Corinthians 1:26. Ask Q8.
- Q9 (do not read verses). Read "Focus on the Meaning."
- *What application will you make:* Q10.

Day Four Study

- Q11—go through these quickly without discussion.
- Q12—Read paragraph and ask first bullet question.
- Q12—second bullet question. Spend time on this. Read "Scriptural Insight."
- Qs13-14 (do not read verses).
- Read paragraph at top of page. Discuss Qs15-16. Read "Think About It."
- Q17—Read 1 Corinthians 10:13. Read "From the Greek."
- Skip paragraph at top of next page. Q18 if you have time.
- Q19 bullets 1 and 2—Break into small groups of 3-4 to share their responses. Give them 3-4 minutes. Discuss Q19 bullet point 3 together.
- Qs20 and 21 (if you have time). Add to chart in Q22. Read "Think About It."
- Read italicized sentence at the end of the lesson.
- Ask what grabbed their attention from the podcast. Highlight what you want to emphasize.
- Pray.

Recommendation: Listen to a worship song such as "Blessed Be the Name of the Lord."

DISCUSSION GUIDE

LESSON 2: PROMISES AND FAITHFULNESS (2 CORINTHIANS 1:12-2:13)

Choose ahead of time which verses from the questions the group will read aloud as you proceed through the discussion. My recommendations are below.

Start with prayer. Review Memory Verse #1 together. Read key verse at top of page.

Day One Study

- Skip reading the passage here. Ask Qs1-2.

Day Two Study

- Read 2 Corinthians 1:12-14.
- Q5—quick answer, no discussion. Read "From the Greek."
- Qs6-8. Read 2 Corinthians 2:1-5. Skip "From the Greek."
- Q9. Discuss 2 Corinthians 1:13—their use of clear and understandable communication. This mirrors what the Spirit does for us (1 Corinthians 2:12)
- Q10—Break into small groups of 3-4 to share their responses. Give them 3-4 minutes. Ask if 1 person wants to briefly share their story.

Day Three Study

- Read 2 Corinthians 1:15-22.
- Q12—quick answers, no discussion. Skip "Scriptural Insight."
- Skip Acts 19:21-22. Read Acts 18:21 and James 4:13-15. Q13. Read first sentence of "Focus on the Meaning."
- Q14 and "Scriptural Insight."
- "What application will you make?" Discuss how to make plans in a godly manner. See podcast notes on page 39.

Day Four Study

- Read 2 Corinthians 1:23-2:13.
- Q16—quick answers, no discussion.
- Qs 17-18. Read "Focus on the Meaning."
- Qs19-21. Skip reading 1 Corinthians 5:1-7. Read "Focus on the Meaning."
- Q22 and last sentence of "Historical Insight."
- Skip Q24 (personal). Ask Q25.
- Add to chart in Q26.
- Read italicized sentence at the end of the lesson.
- Ask what grabbed their attention from the podcast. Highlight what you want to emphasize. Discuss the saying evaluated this week.
- Pray.

Recommendation: Listen to a worship song such as "Build My Life."

THE GOD-DEPENDENT WOMAN

LESSON 3: CONNECT AND IMPART FOR GOD'S GLORY (2 CORINTHIANS 2:14-4:6)

Choose ahead of time which verses from the questions the group will read aloud as you proceed through the discussion. My recommendations are below.

Start with prayer. Review Memory Verse #1 together. Read key verse at top of page.

Day One Study

- Skip reading the passage here. Ask Qs1-3.

Day Two Study

- Read 2 Corinthians 2:14-17.
- Q5—quick answer, no discussion. Read "Think About It."
- Qs6-7 (don't read the verses), "From the Greek," and both "Scriptural Insights." Skip Q8.
- Qs9-10.

Day Three Study

- Read 2 Corinthians 3:1-6. Skip "Historical Insight."
- Q12—quick answers, no discussion. Read "Focus on the Meaning."
- Qs13-14. Don't read the verses in Q14.
- Q15 and "From the Greek." Then discuss Q18.
- For Q17, break into small groups of 3-4 to share their answers to 1st and 3rd bullets.

Day Four Study

- Read 2 Corinthians 3:7-4:6.
- Q20—quick answers, no discussion. Skip "Focus on the Meaning."
- Q21 and "Focus on the Meaning."
- Q22 (don't read the verses). Skip "Scriptural Insight."
- Q23 and "Scriptural Insight."
- Q24. Skip "Scriptural Insight."
- For Q26, break into small groups of 3-4 to share their answers. Ask 1-2 to share with the large group.
- Q27—ask one person to share their answer.
- Add to chart in Q28.
- Read italicized sentence at the end of the lesson.
- Ask what grabbed their attention from the podcast. Highlight what you want to emphasize. Discuss the saying evaluated this week.
- Pray.

> Recommendation: Listen to a worship song such as "Shine, Jesus, Shine"

DISCUSSION GUIDE

LESSON 4: LET GOD'S LIGHT SHINE (2 CORINTHIANS 4:7-5:10)

Choose ahead of time which verses from the questions the group will read aloud as you proceed through the discussion. My recommendations are below.

Start with prayer. Review Memory Verse #1 together. Read key verse at top of page (MV#2).

Opening question (optional): What do you appreciate about being human?

Day One Study

- Skip reading the passage here. Ask Qs1-2.

Day Two Study

- Read 2 Corinthians 4:7-12. Q5—quick answers, no discussion.
- Read "Historical Insight." Qs6-7. Skip "Think About It."
- Qs8-9 and "Focus on the Meaning."
- Q10 is optional.
- Q11. Read "Think About It."
- Discuss the podcast section—"God is bigger than your weaknesses" on page 69.

Day Three Study

- Read 2 Corinthians 4:13-18. Q13—quick answers, no discussion.
- Q14—read Psalm 116:5-10. Read "Think About It."
- Qs15-16.
- Discuss the podcast section—"Endurance as you view purpose and reward" on page 70.
- What application will you make? Read paragraph then discuss Q18. This can be done in small groups of 2-3 then shared in a larger group.

Day Four Study

- Read 2 Corinthians 5:1-10. Q20—quick answers, no discussion.
- Q21.
- Q22. Read 1 Corinthians 15:53-54. Read "Scriptural Insight."
- Q23. Read "Think About It."
- Q24. Ski Q25. Ask Q26. Be sure to read the chart in the "Scriptural Insight."
- Discuss the podcast notes. Highlight what you want to emphasize.
- Discuss the saying evaluated this week.
- Add to chart in Q28.
- Read italicized sentence at the end of the lesson.
- Pray.

Recommendation: Listen to a worship song such as "In Christ Alone."

THE GOD-DEPENDENT WOMAN

LESSON 5: YOUR LIFE HAS PURPOSE (2 CORINTHIANS 5:11-6:10)

Choose ahead of time which verses from the questions the group will read aloud as you proceed through the discussion. My recommendations are below.

Start with prayer. Review Memory Verse #1 and MV #2 together. Read key verse at top of page.

Day One Study

- Skip reading the passage here. Ask Qs1-3.

Day Two Study

- Read 2 Corinthians 5:11-15. Q5—quick answers, no discussion.
- Q6. Read verses.
- Qs7-8 and "Focus on the Meaning."

Day Three Study

- Read 2 Corinthians 5:16-21. Skip Q13.
- Q14 and "Scriptural Insight."
- Q15 and "Scriptural Insight."
- Q16 and "Think About It."
- Q17 and "Scriptural Insight."
- Q18 and "Scriptural Insight."
- Q19 and "Think About It." Skip Q20.

Day Four Study

- Read 2 Corinthians 6:1-10. Q21—quick answers from the text. Skip "From the Greek."
- Q22.
- Q23-24. Read verses in Q23.
- Read paragraph after "What application will you make?"
- For Q25, break into small groups of 3 to share their stories. Give them 3 minutes.
- Ask for 1-2 to share with the larger group.
- Add to chart in Q27.
- Read italicized sentence at the end of the lesson.
- Ask what grabbed their attention from the podcast. Highlight what you want to emphasize. Discuss the saying evaluated this week.
- Pray.

Recommendation: Listen to a worship song such as "Before the Throne of God Above."

DISCUSSION GUIDE

Lesson 6: Open Wide Your Hearts (2 Corinthians 6:11-7:16))

Choose ahead of time which verses from the questions the group will read aloud as you proceed through the discussion. My recommendations are below.

Start with prayer. Review Memory Verse #1 and MV #2 together. Read key verse at top of page.

Day One Study

- Skip reading the passage here. Ask Qs1-2. Optional ask their response to God after reading the passage.

Day Two Study

- Read 2 Corinthians 6:11-7:1. Q5—quick answers.
- Read paragraph under "What Does It Mean?"
- Q6. Skip "Scriptural Insight."
- Skip Qs7-8.
- Qs9 and 10. Spend some time on these situations. Read "Think About It."

Day Three Study

- Read 2 Corinthians 7:2-7. Q12—quick answers.
- Q13.
- Q14 and "From the Greek."
- Q15. Be sure to cover 7:4 is you have not already. This is a totally supernatural response.
- For Q16, break into small groups of 3-4 to share their stories. Give them 3 minutes.

Day Four Study

- Read 2 Corinthians 7:8-16. Q17—quick answers. Read "Think About It."
- Q18.
- Q19. Read "Focus on the Meaning."
- Q20. What we write can have profound consequences. Don't be afraid to cause pain about something that truly matters with the goal of healing the relationship.
- Q21. Read the four steps and the "Think About It."
- Add to chart in Q23.
- Read italicized sentence at the end of the lesson.
- Ask what grabbed their attention from the podcast. Highlight what you want to emphasize. Discuss the saying evaluated this week.
- Pray.

> Recommendation: Listen to a worship song such as "Lord, I Need You."

LESSON 7: GENEROSITY FROM JOY OVERFLOWING (2 CORINTHIANS 8:1-9:15)

Choose ahead of time which verses from the questions the group will read aloud as you proceed through the discussion. My recommendations are below.

Start with prayer. Review MV #1 & MV #2. Introduce MV#3. Read key verse at top of page.

Day One Study

- This is such a long passage. Skip reading the passage here and skip Qs1-4.

Day Two Study

- Read 2 Corinthians 8:1-10. Q5—quick answers.
- Q6. Read "Think About It."
- Qs7-8 (including 1 Corinthians 1:5-7). Read "Scriptural Insight."
- Q9. Skip Q10.
- Tithing and the grace of giving: Read "Scriptural Insight."
- Q11.

Day Three Study

- Read 2 Corinthians 8:10-24. Q12—quick answers. The Galatian churches were also collecting an offering. Skip "Scriptural Insight."
- Read paragraph then ask Q13.
- Q14 and "Scriptural Insight."
- Q15. Skip Q16.
- Q17.
- Skip "Historical Insight," and skip Qs18-19.

Day Four Study

- Read 2 Corinthians 9:1-15. Q20—quick answers. Read "From the Greek."
- Q21 and "Think About It."
- Q22 and "Scriptural Insight."
- Skip Qs23-25.
- Add to chart in Q26.
- Discuss the podcast. Highlight what you want to emphasize.
- Discuss the saying evaluated this week.
- Read italicized sentence at the end of the lesson.
- Pray.

> Recommendation: Listen to a worship song such as "Blessed Be the Name of the Lord."

DISCUSSION GUIDE

LESSON 8: TEARING DOWN WALLS (2 CORINTHIANS 10:1-18)

Choose ahead of time which verses from the questions the group will read aloud as you proceed through the discussion. My recommendations are below.

Start with prayer. Review MV #2 and #3. Read key verse at top of page.

Day One Study

- Skip reading the passage. Ask Qs1-2.

Day Two Study

- Skip reading the passage. Point out "I, Paul" in verse 1 and read "Scriptural Insight."
- Q5—quick answers. Read "Historical Insight."
- Q6, including "Focus on the Meaning."
- Q7 and "Think About It."
- Q8. Read "Focus on the Greek" and "Think About It."
- Qs9-10. Skip "Focus on the Meaning."
- Qs12 -13.

Day Three Study

- Read 2 Corinthians 10:7-11. Read paragraph at top of page.
- Q14 and "Scriptural Insight."
- Qs15-17 and "Think About It."
- Q18 if time.
- Qs19-20.

Day Four Study

- Read 2 Corinthians 10:12-18. Read "Historical Insight."
- Q22. Read "Focus on the Meaning."
- Q23. Read "Think About It."
- Q24 and "Focus on the Meaning."
- Qs25-27.
- Add to chart in Q29.
- Ask what grabbed their attention from the podcast. Highlight what you want to emphasize.
- Discuss the saying evaluated this week.
- Read italicized sentence at the end of the lesson.
- Pray

Recommendation: Listen to a worship song such as "Lord, I Need You."

THE GOD-DEPENDENT WOMAN

LESSON 9: LIVE TO SERVE CHRIST THROUGH ANYTHING (2 CORINTHIANS 11:1-33)

Choose ahead of time which verses from the questions the group will read aloud as you proceed through the discussion. My recommendations are below.

Start with prayer. Review MV #2 and #3. Read key verse at top of page.

Day One Study

- Skip reading the passage. Ask Qs1-2.

Day Two Study

- Read 2 Corinthians 11:1-15. Q5—quick answers.
- Q6 and "Focus on the Meaning."
- Q7 and "Think About It."
- Qs8-9 and each "Scriptural Insight."
- Qs11-12.

Day Three Study

- Read 2 Corinthians 11:16-21. Q14—quick answers.
- Q15 and "Think About It."
- Q16.
- Read "From the Greek" and ask Q18.
- Q19.

Day Four Study

- Read 2 Corinthians 11:22-33. Q21—quick answers, skipping the chart.
- Skip Q22.
- Qs23-24 and "Think About It."
- Skip Q25. Don't read "Think About It."
- Q26. Discuss podcast at this point.
- Skip Qs27-28.
- Add to chart in Q29.
- Read italicized sentence at the end of the lesson.
- Pray

> Recommendation: Listen to a worship song such as "You Are God Alone."

DISCUSSION GUIDE

LESSON 10: DEPENDENT LIVING IS POWERFUL (2 CORINTHIANS 12:1-21)

Choose ahead of time which verses from the questions the group will read aloud as you proceed through the discussion. My recommendations are below.

Start with prayer. Review MV #2. Read key verse at top of page.

Day One Study

- Skip reading the passage. Ask Qs1-2.

Day Two Study

- Read 2 Corinthians 12:1-10. Read "Focus on the Meaning."
- Ask Q5—quick answers. Read "Historical Insight."
- Qs6-7 and "Think About It."
- Q8 and "From the Greek." Spend time thinking through these questions.
- Qs9-13.
- Qs14-15. Turn Q16 into prayer requests.
- Ask if anyone has a creative response to the Lord's grace.

Day Three Study

- Read 2 Corinthians 12:11-18. Ask Q18—quick answers.
- Qs19-20.
- Qs21-22 and "Focus on the Meaning."
- Qs23-24.

Day Four Study

- Read 2 Corinthians 12:19-21. Ask Q25—quick answers. Read "Focus on the Meaning."
- Q26.
- Qs27-28.
- Add to chart in Q31.
- Ask what grabbed their attention from the podcast. Highlight what you want to emphasize.
- Read italicized sentence at the end of the lesson.
- Pray

Recommendation: Listen to a worship song such as "Lord, I Need You."

THE GOD-DEPENDENT WOMAN

LESSON 11: CHRIST IS ALL WE NEED FOR LIFE (2 CORINTHIANS 13:1-14)

Choose ahead of time which verses from the questions the group will read aloud as you proceed through the discussion. My recommendations are below.

Start with prayer. Review MV #1, 2, and 3. Read key verse at top of page. Read paragraphs on page 167.

Day One Study

- Skip reading the passage. Ask Qs1-2.

Day Two Study

- Read 2 Corinthians 13:1-4. Ask Q5. Read "Focus on the Meaning."
- Qs6-7 and "Focus on the Meaning."
- Qs8-9 and "Think About It."

Day Three Study

- Read 2 Corinthians 13:5-10. Ask Q11.
- Read "From the Greek." Ask Q12.
- Read "From the Greek." Ask Qs13-14.
- Ask Q15. Read the paragraph that comes after it. Talk about lack of prayer being a sign of self-sufficiency.

Day Four Study

- Read 2 Corinthians 13:11-14.
- Q16.
- Q17 and "Historical Insight."
- Q18 and "Historical Insight."
- Q19—Read v. 14 together.
- Q20 and "Scriptural Insight."
- Add to chart in Q21. Point out chart in "Resources" section and suggest they add their own to it.
- Discuss "Famous Last Words."
- Discuss the saying evaluated this week.
- Ask what grabbed their attention from the podcast. Highlight what you want to emphasize.
- Read italicized sentence at the end of the lesson.
- Pray

Recommendation: Listen to a worship song such as "Forever He Is Glorified."

Sources

1. Biblical Hermeneutics Stack Exchange
2. Dane C. Ortlund, *Why Study the Book of 2 Corinthians?* posted online August 2, 2016
3. Dr. Sandra Glahn, *"Biblical Womanhood": What is a Woman?*
4. *Dr. Tom Constable's Notes on 2 Corinthians 2017 Edition*
5. Heather Zempel, *Community Is Messy*
6. Jim Cymbala, *Fresh Wind, Fresh Fire*
7. John Newton, *Advent for Restless Hearts*
8. Joni Eareckson Tada, *Just Between Us,* Fall 2018
9. Kelly Minter, *All Things New*
10. Major Ian Thomas, *The Saving Life of Christ*
11. *NIV Study Bible*
12. Steve Hixon
13. *The Bible Knowledge Commentary (New Testament),* Walvoord and Zuck

www.ingramcontent.com/pod-product-compliance
Lightning Source LLC
Chambersburg PA
CBHW060421010526
44118CB00017B/2304